Loose Parts in Action

Lisa Daly

Redleaf Press®
www.redleafpress.org
800-423-8309

Published by Redleaf Press
10 Yorkton Court
St. Paul, MN 55117
www.redleafpress.org

First edition 2023
Cover design by Erin Kirk
Cover photographs by Lisa Daly
Interior design by Michelle Lee Lagerroos
Typeset in Servus Slab, Futura PT, and Cabin Sketch
Interior photos by Lisa Daly; interior illustrations by Michelle Lee Lagerroos
Printed in the United States of America

Library of Congress Cataloging-in-Publication Data
Names: Daly, Lisa, author.
Title: Loose parts in action : the essential how-to guide / by Lisa Daly.
Description: First edition. | St. Paul, MN : Redleaf Press, 2023. |
Summary: "Take loose parts from inspiration to implementation with this practical, easy-to-use loose parts manual. Loose Parts in Action provides specific instructions and a step-by-step process for infusing loose parts into early learning environments, to make implementing loose parts simple and approachable for educators in programs of all types"-- Provided by publisher.
Identifiers: LCCN 2023007469 (print) | LCCN 2023007470 (ebook) | ISBN 9781605547947 (paperback) | ISBN 9781605547954 (ebook)
Subjects: LCSH: Play. | Early childhood education--Activity programs. | Creative activities and seat work.
Classification: LCC LB1139.35.P55 D373 2023 (print) | LCC LB1139.35.P55 (ebook) | DDC 372.21--dc23/eng/20230303
LC record available at https://lccn.loc.gov/2023007469
LC ebook record available at https://lccn.loc.gov/2023007470

Printed on acid-free paper U25-06

To all who desire to nurture children's curiosity, competence, independence, resilience, critical thinking, resourcefulness, imagination, and creativity.

Contents

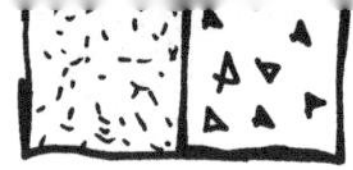

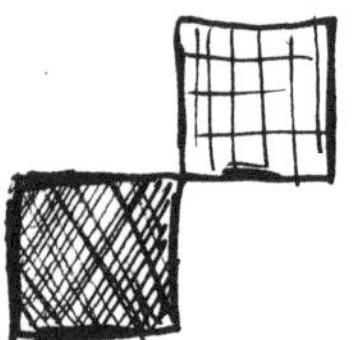

Acknowledgments

Writing this loose parts guide and capturing all that is important for implementing loose parts into early childhood programs involved the guidance of many people.

This book is better thanks to Kellie Bliss, Nicole Hall, Jenna Knight, Clara Nakai, Lindsey Shafer, and Cheri Quishenbery, who provided invaluable expertise about areas where educators struggle in implementing loose parts. Your input provided insight into educators' understandings and challenges and served as a blueprint for content.

I am grateful for Samantha Straker, Allie Armstrong, Jennifer Pearl, Kim Thode, and Lisa Thomas at Wintonbury Early Childhood Magnet School for your strong commitment to continuous improvement, open-mindedness, and wholeheartedness. You have the gift of being able to self-assess and determine what is working and why. Your thoughtful questions from your personal experiences inspired relevant content throughout the book.

A very special thank-you to Dr. Joyce Yang, Dr. Deepa Aier, and Sheree Berry-Todd of the Virginia Preschool Initiative (VPI) for having the vision to provide high-quality early childhood programs for children and families and meaningful learning opportunities for educators. For the VPI center-based and family child care educators, thank you for your active participation in loose parts cohort groups and your ability to take risks as you tried new options and committed yourselves to implementing program changes.

Special thanks to Melissa York, who improved the manuscript with her attention to detail and ability to provide clarity and completeness. You challenged me to look at content through a different lens.

I want to extend my gratitude to my husband, Dan, for always being there and for his insights, guidance, never-ending love, and support.

Finally, to all those who have been a part of my loose parts journey, without your experiences and support, this book would not exist.

INTRODUCTION

Why Loose Parts in Action?

Ever since I cowrote the Loose Parts series beginning eight years ago, the number one question I hear in all the loose parts presentations and consultations I do is "How do you put loose parts into action?" After completing an online presentation titled "Designing Indoor Environments with Loose Parts," I debriefed with the agency team. One program analyst commented, "This was absolutely the best presentation ever. Don't get me wrong. Your books are beautiful, but many directors just give teachers your books without any guidance or instructions. Teachers find the photos inspiring but are overwhelmed and don't know where to begin or what to do. Your presentation tonight walked everyone through a step-by-step process for creating a loose parts environment. I wish that all teachers could experience your guidance."

Her comments made me reflect on an idea I had been contemplating for quite some time: to create a loose parts how-to instruction manual or handbook. There is a lot of rich material in the Loose Parts book series about what loose parts are, as well as their value and significance, but the books contain limited how-to information.

Throughout my years of researching and implementing loose parts, I have discovered wide variation in educators' knowledge and acceptance of loose parts. Some educators have a solid understanding, and others are very open to learning more. Some have tried implementing loose parts but have been unsuccessful for a variety of reasons. Failed attempts have resulted in frustration, confusion, and in some instances elimination of loose parts. Some educators have misconceptions about loose parts, leading to inappropriate

implementation or preventing the introduction of loose parts play altogether. Some are overwhelmed or intimidated by loose parts.

Whatever an educator's experience with or understanding of loose parts, there is a lot to know and learn. Loose parts are both simple and complex. Loose parts themselves are simple, open-ended materials. However, the process of implementing them into the environment is complex. It's not a matter of simply placing loose parts on a shelf and then expecting children to discover them and engage in sustained, creative play. A lot goes into selecting, staging, introducing, and maintaining loose parts, as well as supporting, encouraging, and sustaining children's interest in them.

This guidebook is designed as a handy reference to complement the Loose Parts book series, a tool for implementing loose parts into your early learning program. With valuable text, helpful suggestions, reflections, and action prompts, this guide takes educators through a step-by-step process of putting loose parts into action. There is no timeline in this guide, so you may go at your own pace.

What's the Purpose of *Loose Parts in Action*?

Over the years, I have supported hundreds of educators in creating loose parts environments. When it comes to transforming spaces, the educators with whom I work are often stumped about where to begin, uncertain about what to do and how to do it, lacking inspiration, or unable to visualize creative solutions. With guidance and support in navigating the implementation process, environments are transformed into incredible learning labs and educators are better prepared to support children's learning. Transformed environments bring immense joy and satisfaction for educators, children, and families. I truly cannot put into words the positive impact a loose parts environment has on everyone, and this effect continues and grows deeper over time. My desire is to make the knowledge and expertise I have gleaned over the years available to all educators, not just the ones I mentor.

Here is what *Loose Parts in Action* is designed to do:

- Construct deeper understandings of loose parts
- Help educators successfully and effectively put loose parts into action
- Break down the implementation of loose parts into an easy-to-follow way
- Increase children's opportunities to play with loose parts
- Serve as a practical resource for improving the quality of children's learning
- Provide a deeper dive into strategies for maintaining a thriving loose parts program
- Cultivate reflective practices

Loose Parts in Action is for educators who are doing these things:

- Teaching in center- and home-based programs
- Influencing the operation and direction of early care and education programs, such as administrators and decision makers
- Working with infants, toddlers, and preschoolers
- Seeking to create rich, meaningful learning experiences
- Pursuing ways to implement loose parts into their program
- Wanting to increase children's engagement, collaboration, and independence while limiting negative behavior

How to Use *Loose Parts in Action*

Begin with the loose parts overview in chapter 1, which offers a summary of loose parts and their value. This foundational information is important as there will be times when you will need to articulate and justify the value of loose parts to families and perhaps administrators. Educators can help families understand why loose parts play is essential for young children's learning and development and how it positions children for future success.

Loose Parts in Action is organized into chapters that walk you through how to implement loose parts into your environment. Designed as a gradual implementation process, it proceeds step-by-step in meaningful increments. Each chapter tackles a specific aspect of the implementation process, from preparing the way to facilitating loose parts play. The final chapter addresses common concerns and challenges related to loose parts and directs you to more detailed information contained within the earlier chapters.

This guide is not designed as a quick how-to manual to flip through and immediately implement steps. I encourage you to take your time in following the chapters and action steps in sequence. The actionable advice is intended to promote the greatest opportunity for successful loose parts implementation.

Reflections: Throughout the guide are reflections designed for you to consider, understand, and gain lessons from your experiences. "Reflect" encourages you to ponder your personal feelings, attitudes, beliefs, and experiences. These prompts may ask you to reflect on how something currently is and what you can do differently. Journaling lines are provided for you to record your reflections directly in this guide. I highly encourage you to do the reflections and carefully think about what you write. Reflections can help you become more insightful and transform your thinking, teaching approaches, and responses to challenges. Your writing will also serve as documentation of your journey. As you process new concepts into different perspectives, you may feel uncomfortable, frustrated, and challenged. Know that this is typical as you try to integrate new information.

The Reflect prompts are to encourage you to do the following:

- Look at your current program, practices, circumstances, and environment
- Consider changes you would like to see
- Ponder what you have learned that you did not know before
- Identify how your perspective has changed
- Express how you can use knowledge gained
- Integrate theory and ideas
- Determine the best way to move forward

Action plans: Action plans ask you to identify tasks to help you achieve a single intention, such as collecting loose parts or clearing a learning area. It can be overwhelming to think of transforming an entire indoor or outdoor classroom to a loose parts environment. Action plans give you a framework for thinking about how you will successfully accomplish each task along the way in a mindful order. Having plans will clarify the tasks you must complete, the resources you require, and the timeline you will follow, if desired.

Action steps: Action steps are the identifiable tasks of action plans, tasks for you to complete to accomplish your goal of infusing loose parts into your program. They are concrete and comprehensive and will move you forward in achieving your goal. Check them off your list when completed.

My hope is that this guide provides the knowledge and understanding you need to effectively infuse loose parts into your program. May you discover the enormous potential loose parts have in expanding children's thinking and investigative play. May the practical teaching and implementation strategies get you started with loose parts play today.

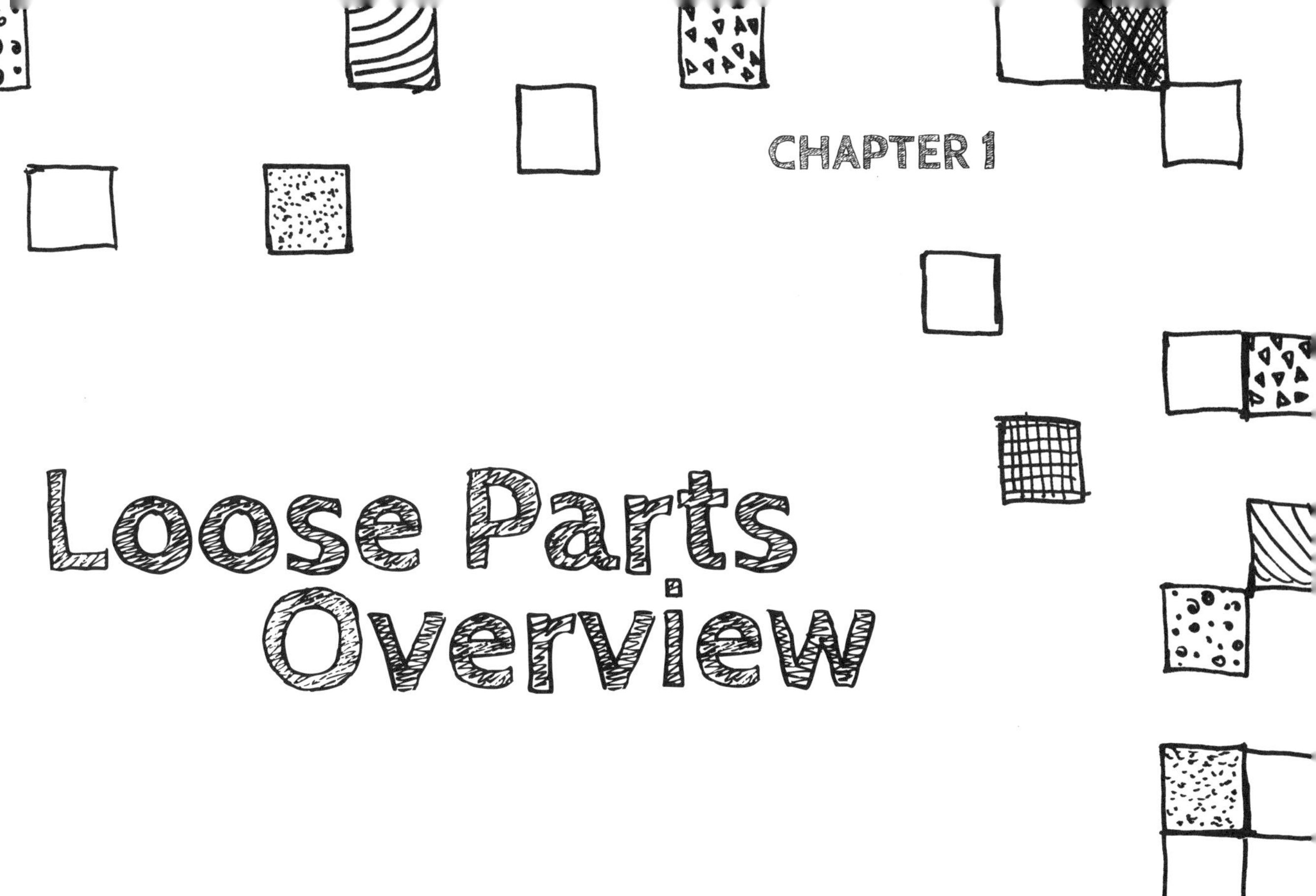

CHAPTER 1

Loose Parts Overview

Loose parts are open-ended materials that children can use in countless ways. Their nondescript nature allows children to decide what they are and change their purpose as often as they like. For example, four-year-old Erica might turn a piece of driftwood into a car, wand, raft, cell phone, or food. She might use it to mix sand and water together or draw lines in the dirt. She might use it along with seashells to make a creative design. The possibilities are endless.

Commercial toys, on the other hand, typically have a single purpose. For example, a horse figurine is a horse. Rarely does a child pick up a horse and pretend that it something else or use it for stirring, building, or drawing. Some toys, such as blocks, are considered loose parts, but most children's toys are designed with an intent that leaves little to the imagination. Additionally, commercial toys often control the child rather than the child controlling the toy. Buttons or levers are pushed to elicit a prescribed result. Children do not have the opportunity to make the item do what they desire. These types of toys become boring very quickly.

One of our challenges as adults is that we have lots of experiences with items, and our minds tend to process only their intended purposes. For example, we see a napkin ring as an item for holding a napkin, but when infants see a napkin ring, they explore the ring to find its most interesting property.

REFLECT

Describe a time when you observed a child using an open-ended item in a nonconventional way, such as a piece of wood as a cell phone. What was your response?

____

____

____

____

____

____

____

____

They may be captivated by the sounds that it can make, its trajectory when dropped, its rotation as it rolls across the floor, or the fact that it fits on their fingers. We can foster children's development and learning by providing open-ended materials.

Why Are Loose Parts So Appealing?

The availability, versatility, economic feasibility, sustainability, and attractiveness of loose parts make them the perfect open-ended items for children's play. The undefined nature of loose parts allows for maximum creative use.

Availability

Loose parts are readily available. Take a walk in nature to discover acorns or fall leaves carpeting the ground. Open cupboard drawers and cabinets to reveal coasters, bowls, wooden thread spools, or towels. Walk down the aisles of a big-box store and discover discarded cardboard molding. Once you start looking, you will be amazed at how many free loose parts there are. Once you have found them, you will be excited to place them in the classroom environment and see what children do with them.

Versatility

Children of all ages, stages, temperaments, learning modalities, and abilities can successfully engage in rich, in-depth loose parts experiences. The open-ended nature of loose parts accommodates the developmental levels, capabilities, and ages of all children. One nice aspect of loose parts is that since materials are appropriate for all children, they do not need to be adjusted or

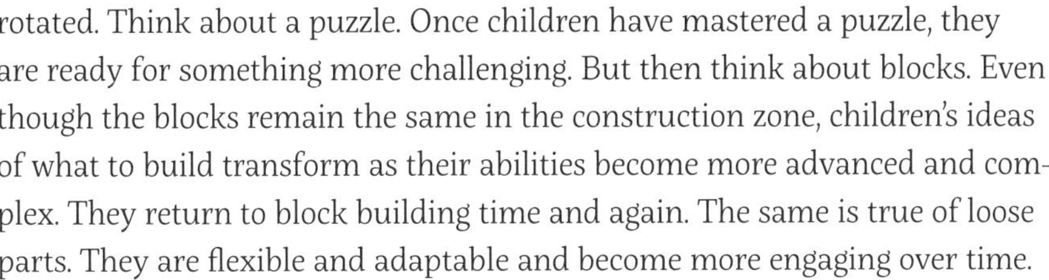

rotated. Think about a puzzle. Once children have mastered a puzzle, they are ready for something more challenging. But then think about blocks. Even though the blocks remain the same in the construction zone, children's ideas of what to build transform as their abilities become more advanced and complex. They return to block building time and again. The same is true of loose parts. They are flexible and adaptable and become more engaging over time.

Economic Feasibility

Most loose parts are found, free, upcycled materials. They are natural elements such as pine cones and seedpods and manufactured materials like plastic caps, tin cans, and cardboard boxes. Take time to learn about free resources in your community. For example, there may be a carpentry shop that gives away scrap wood. Some loose parts are inexpensive purchases from discount, thrift, or hardware stores. You can also find economical loose parts at garage sales, flea markets, and trading posts. There is no need to purchase loose parts from big commercial companies that charge a lot of money for a collection of items. You can put the collection together yourself for little or no charge.

Sustainability

Loose parts are often obtained by upcycling materials headed for landfill. One way to help children learn about their own impact on the environment is through the reuse of materials. Finding discarded items and repurposing them to create new play possibilities is a central component of loose parts philosophy. Play and learning can be enriched with unwanted materials.

Attractiveness

Loose parts are visually appealing. Consider the natural beauty of a collection of seashells, sea glass, and driftwood. The colors complement each other, and their textures beckon you to run your fingers over them. A bowl of buttons entices you to dive your hand in deep and pull out a fistful. Surrounding children and educators with aesthetically appealing loose parts in interesting textures, colors, and sounds enhances the beauty of play spaces. Environments affect how we feel, think, and behave.

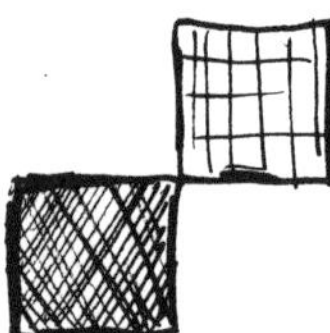

Flexibility

The very nature of loose parts is flexibility and unlimited possibilities. They may be investigated, transported, transformed, combined, and manipulated. They may be used for creating, designing, representing, pretending, constructing, exploring, and patterning. Having different types of loose parts easily accessible in each play zone affords diverse play opportunities and appeals to children's varying interests. When children are presented with loose parts and flexible furnishings, they engage in a wide variety of rich experiences that cultivates their learning and development.

Fun for Everyone

To me, the fun and excitement of loose parts is discovering them! Collecting loose parts yourself does take time and energy, but it is a thrill when you come across a great find. It is also a wonderful way to engage families and communities. Often when I find something at a garage sale, in nature, or in a store aisle, individuals ask me what I am going to do with the items. When I explain that I am using the materials for children's play, their faces light up and they eagerly contribute free materials. Often they have ideas for other things the children would like and tell me stories of what they played with as a child. What loose parts lie in your future?

REFLECT

What do you find most appealing about loose parts?

____

____

____

____

____

____

____

____

Types of Loose Parts

There is a wide variety of loose parts both natural and manufactured. The following are some of the loose parts I've seen that often get a great response. What ideas can you add to my list?

Natural

Natural loose parts are loose parts collected from nature. Here are some ideas: stones, seashells, sticks, pine cones, leaves, bark, tree cookies, flowers, seedpods.

Metal

Children gravitate to metal loose parts perhaps because they are familiar items used by adults. They may also be drawn to sounds they make or find them alluring because they are often inaccessible. Here are some metal loose parts to collect or purchase: washers, nuts, bolts, tin cans, napkin and canning rings, keys, pots and pans, hubcaps.

Plastic

Since plastic lasts forever in the environment and plastic pollution is a global problem, it is a good thing anytime plastic items can be upcycled for another use. Here are some plastic loose parts: bottle caps, film canisters (now vanishing; hold on to these useful little containers tightly!), tape dispenser reels, beakers, cylinders, cups, bowls.

Wood

Unfinished wood products are beautiful and simple. Wood examples include thread spools, napkin rings, wood rings, checkers and other game pieces, wheels, pegs, blocks, scrap wood, clothespins.

Paper

Paper recycling saves landfill space and lessens damaging effects on our environment. Here are some paper loose parts ideas: cardboard (boxes, tubes, rings, and molding), postcards, envelopes, paper cups, paint swatches.

Textiles

Often home cabinets and cupboards are filled with extra, unused, or worn fabrics. Here are some textile loose parts to collect: fabric, yarn, ribbons, upholstery samples, scarves, rope, cloth napkins.

Glass

Educators' comfort in using glass items with young children varies from program to program. Some programs feel the possibility of breaking glass is a safety hazard and do not allow any glass materials. Other programs support the use of glass items and report that children learn very quickly how to control their movements to prevent breakage. Handling glass materials offers a lesson in caring for fragile items. These programs cite multiple advantages for using glass that far outweigh disadvantages. I encourage you to research why glass and other breakable objects are part of the learning experiences offered in Montessori and Reggio Emilia–inspired programs. Here are some glass loose parts to collect or purchase: sea glass; empty jars; glass tiles; glass stones for vases, crafts, and gardens in varying sizes, colors, and shapes.

Benefits of Loose Parts

As children manipulate, experiment, investigate, construct, and deconstruct with loose parts, their play and learning expand. Intriguing loose parts found throughout indoor and outdoor environments offer deeper play and learning possibilities. Playing with varied, open-ended loose parts nurtures children's critical thinking, inventiveness, creativity, and imagination—all important characteristics for future school success. Using loose parts in your program fosters essential domains of children's learning and development—social-emotional, language and literacy, cognitive, physical, and creative.

Enhancing Social and Emotional Competencies

Having the freedom to use loose parts as desired builds self-confidence as children experience the results of their own choices, actions, and accomplishments. When children repeatedly use the same loose parts over time, they gain a sense of surety and competence.

Social skills such as sharing, contributing, leading, and following develop as children share space and loose parts, show consideration for and cooperation with others, and help one another. Play in a construction zone, for example, offers social opportunities for children to cooperate, communicate, and problem solve as they build. When collaborating on building a structure such as a skyscraper, children must negotiate and work through problems and disagreements that arise.

Emotional competencies of perseverance, initiative, independence, and self-regulation are fostered as children spend long periods of time doing something that piques their curiosity and is intrinsically motivating. Children also use loose parts to express thoughts and feelings that seem overwhelming or unmanageable. For example, Aiden's family had to evacuate their home because of a fire. For a week he repeatedly reenacted the evacuation and the damage to his home with loose parts.

Note: Directors and educators who have transformed their programs into loose parts environments have overwhelmingly reported to me that collaboration and cooperation among children immediately increased while disagreements, fighting, arguing, and physical aggression reduced substantially.

Enhancing Language and Literacy Competencies

Playing with loose parts is an optimal way to develop language, communication, and literacy competencies because it allows children to practice language in a meaningful context. Children can use loose parts to express what is significant to them. As children tinker with language, they discover the power of words. They learn that language can express ideas or feelings, argue a point, convey information, evoke a response, and initiate or maintain contact with people. A magical thing happens as children experience loose parts. They automatically begin to talk freely to others about their ideas and what they are doing. Children begin to connect language, objects, and actions to create increasingly complex story lines and adapt their language to reflect different perspectives and roles. Children often use loose parts for storytelling

and imaginative play. Vocabulary increases as children experience a variety of loose parts for exploring, constructing, imagining, and creating.

Literacy skills develop through loose parts play. It takes imagination and creativity for a child to pretend that a loose part represents something else. This is called *symbolic representation*, which means using one object or symbol to represent another. This skill is necessary for learning to read and write, because words are symbols or representations of thoughts and objects.

Enhancing Cognitive Competencies

Scientific inquiry skills: Through play with loose parts, children develop thinking, inquiry, and prediction skills. They recognize cause-and-effect relationships such as what happens when water is added to dirt. Loose parts create science-rich environments for children to engage, notice, wonder, and question. Scientific inquiry expands as children transform, transfer, and transport materials in an open-ended way. As children build progressively complex block structures, they gain a deeper understanding of science concepts such as stability, gravity, and balance. Like scientists, children develop hypotheses, try them out, and experiment with materials through trial and error. The science inquiry skills children acquire through loose parts play equip them to attain deeper understanding of science concepts.

Scientific Inquiry Skills Fostered through Loose Parts Play		
Analyzing	Communicating	Discovering
Evaluating	Examining	Experimenting
Exploring	Hypothesizing	Inferring
Inquiring	Inventing	Investigating
Observing	Pondering	Predicting
Problem Solving	Processing	Questioning
Reflecting	Researching	Testing
Tinkering	Understanding Cause and Effect	Wondering

Math skills: Young children naturally construct math concepts while playing with loose parts. Acorns, seashells, eucalyptus pods, pine cones, and sea glass encourage patterning, ordering, comparing, contrasting, classifying, counting, and measuring. Using loose parts, children develop other math concepts, such as symmetry,

REFLECT

What natural loose parts could you add to your program to foster mathematical learning?

Math Skills Fostered through Loose Parts Play		
Classifying	Comparing/Contrasting	Counting
Estimating	Exploring Position and Location	Exploring Shapes
Matching	Measuring (Volume, Weight, Length)	Ordering
Patterning	Sorting	Subitizing
Understanding One-to-One Correspondence	Understanding Part/Whole	Understanding Quantity

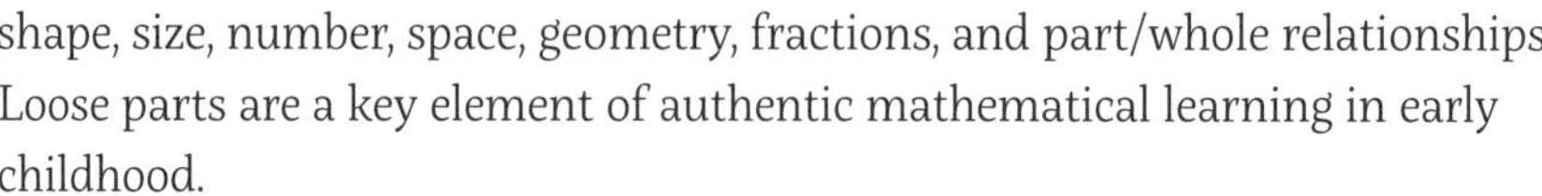

shape, size, number, space, geometry, fractions, and part/whole relationships. Loose parts are a key element of authentic mathematical learning in early childhood.

Enhancing Physical Competencies

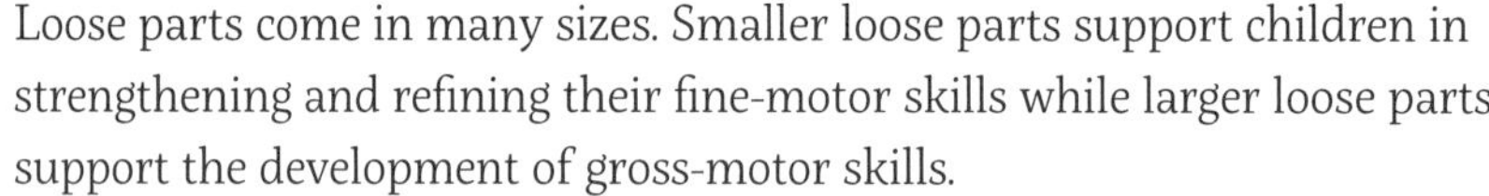

Loose parts come in many sizes. Smaller loose parts support children in strengthening and refining their fine-motor skills while larger loose parts support the development of gross-motor skills.

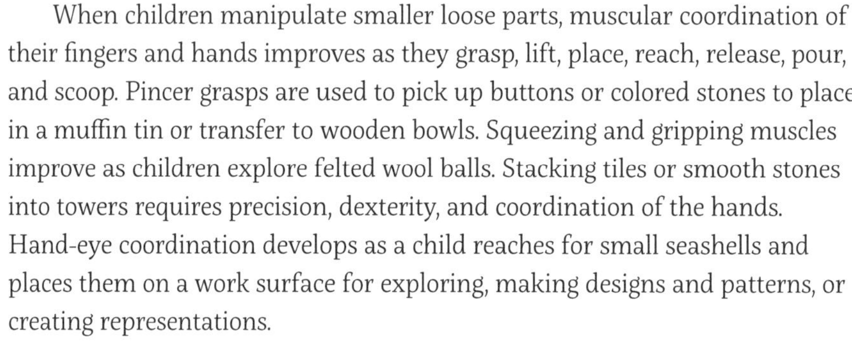

When children manipulate smaller loose parts, muscular coordination of their fingers and hands improves as they grasp, lift, place, reach, release, pour, and scoop. Pincer grasps are used to pick up buttons or colored stones to place in a muffin tin or transfer to wooden bowls. Squeezing and gripping muscles improve as children explore felted wool balls. Stacking tiles or smooth stones into towers requires precision, dexterity, and coordination of the hands. Hand-eye coordination develops as a child reaches for small seashells and places them on a work surface for exploring, making designs and patterns, or creating representations.

Play with large loose parts such as tires, crates, long planks, and heavy rocks fosters large-motor development. These play experiences are typically outdoors. Children use large-motor skills for transporting, arranging, stacking, rolling, constructing, deconstructing, and balancing. Muscle strength is needed to push, pull, move, and position heavy tires and to build big structures for climbing and balancing. Large loose parts allow children freedom to move materials and redesign spaces while fostering gross-motor skills.

Enhancing Creative Competencies

Space, unlimited time, and access to intriguing loose parts invite children to engage in creative play. Because of the open-ended nature of loose parts, imaginative possibilities are infinite. Creative intelligence is the ability to go beyond what currently exists to create innovative ideas. Children tend to be very creative, perhaps because of their innate curiosities. A child can discover multiple ways to use a spoon, while an adult thinks of it only for eating.

Using loose parts for art enhances children's creative expression, originality, and individuality. There is not a right or wrong way to create. Art with

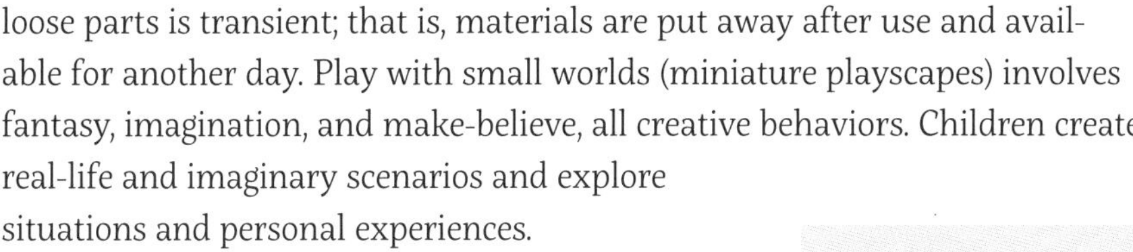

loose parts is transient; that is, materials are put away after use and available for another day. Play with small worlds (miniature playscapes) involves fantasy, imagination, and make-believe, all creative behaviors. Children create real-life and imaginary scenarios and explore situations and personal experiences.

Creative-thinking skills may be seen anywhere in the environment as children tinker with loose parts in new ways. Creativity is not just seen with art, music, or storytelling, but also in a beautiful leaf design on a tree round, an interesting representation of apple pie at the clay table, an innovative way of combining materials in the mud kitchen, and transparent cups balanced on the light table. The flexible nature of loose parts affords children opportunities to investigate solutions and creatively solve problems.

Using loose parts in your program will foster children's capacities across every developmental domain and develop valuable skills in multiple interest areas such as art, science, math, literacy, blocks, dramatic play, sensory exploration, and music. As children work and play with loose parts, they acquire lifelong learning to thrive in the future.

REFLECT

Describe your thoughts about using loose parts to foster children's competencies. Do you support a play-based philosophy or direct instruction as the best way for children to learn skills? Justify your reasoning.

____

____

____

____

____

____

____

____

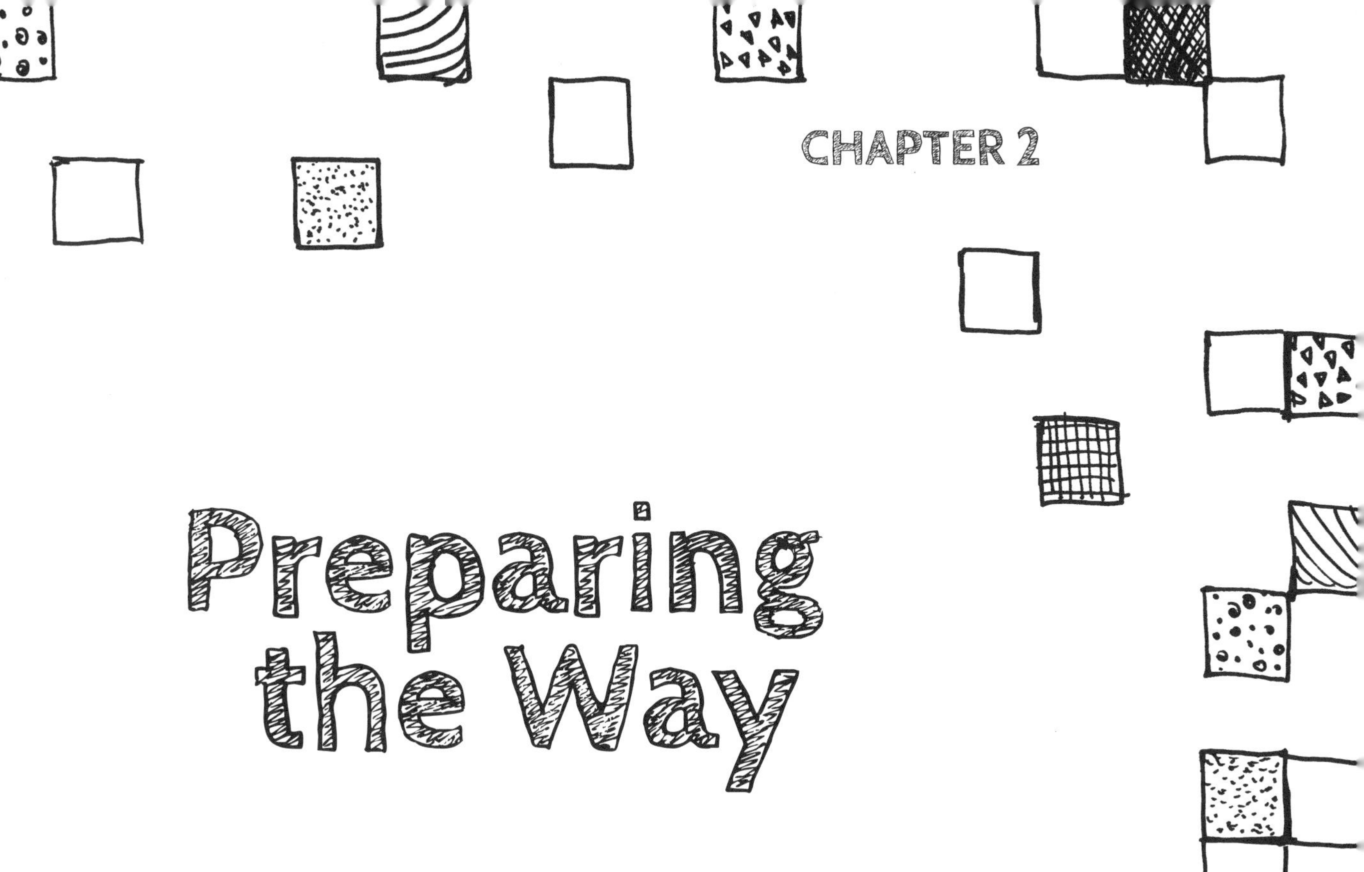

CHAPTER 2

Preparing the Way

My first introduction to loose parts came as I learned about the Reggio Emilia approach. I became fascinated with the Italian pedagogistas' value of using found materials to convey and communicate thoughts, feelings, and understandings. I next encountered Simon Nicholson's concept of loose parts. His work gave context to what I believed: that play with open-ended materials is vital to nurture children's curiosity, competence, independence, resilience, critical thinking, resourcefulness, imagination, and creativity.

Looking back on my years of teaching young children, I recall the materials that most invited children's engagement and sustained focus were unrestricted, as blocks, sand, and water are. This was also true of my own children. They were involved for hours in our backyard using found materials like stones, sticks, flowers, pine cones, and leaves.

These experiences taught me that introducing educators to loose parts was an ideal way to foster their understanding of children's potential for discovery, investigation, and creative expression. Loose parts are foundational for transforming children's learning and development and adults' understanding of meaningful learning.

REFLECT

Take a moment to reflect on the materials in your indoor and outdoor setting that invite the most engagement and sustained focus. List the items or areas that children come back to repeatedly each day.

____

____

____

____

____

____

____

____

Understand the Allure of Loose Parts

Loose parts are magical: they are powerful, captivating, mysteriously attractive, and fascinating. Loose parts are so alluring that in no time children are actively investigating their qualities and possibilities. Perhaps it is because children are instinctively driven to explore and discover, or because they have an unquenchable curiosity, propelled by wonder and an immense capacity for engagement. Consider how children are sometimes more enamored with the box a toy comes in than the toy itself. Observing children at play with loose parts quickly validates how enthralling they are. Once educators see them in action, they too become advocates and avid collectors of loose parts, as teacher Cheri discovered. Cheri had invested a lot of time, energy, effort, and resources in creating a firefighter theme for the children in her program. She made hoses with an old garden hose, oxygen tanks with empty juice bottles and duct tape as straps, and fire extinguishers with plastic spray bottles coated with red tape. She painted a playhouse to resemble a fire station. She purchased fire helmets, flashlights, and jackets, and even made pretend fire with red, orange, and yellow fabric. The children carried out firefighter play, but over time their interest diminished.

As we began to work together, Cheri and I had several reflective conversations about the firefighter setup. From where did the idea of playing firefighter come? What type of actions did the children engage in while playing firefighter? What did children find exciting or satisfying about the play?

Cheri had an aha moment after she shared with me that the children never engaged in any other type of dramatic play with all the wonderful props. I challenged Cheri to take away all the firefighter props and put scarves in their place. She was hesitant because of all the time and money she had

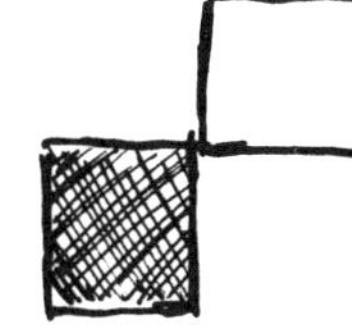

invested but was willing to give it a try. She was also convinced that the children would ask for all the materials to come back. To her amazement, upon removing the materials, not one child asked about the firefighter props. Over the next few months, the children's dramatic play evolved. Scarves were used as superhero capes; bird, butterfly, and fairy wings; veils for brides; skirts for dancing; baby blankets; picnic blankets; and in many other creative ways. Cheri saw firsthand how having loose parts dramatically changed children's creativity, problem solving, and imagination.

Transform Your Thinking

Infusing an environment with loose parts involves a transformation in thinking to embrace a curriculum approach that involves play-based learning. Play-based learning presents opportunities for children to interact with open-ended materials, people, and the environment actively and creatively. This is a shift away from curriculum themes and standard early childhood toys. Play with loose parts looks different, and that can put educators into a temporary state of disequilibrium, particularly if they are used to teaching a specific way.

REFLECT

What play-based learning opportunities are available in your program? What items are theme based in your program? How might they be limiting children's imaginations?

___

___

___

___

___

___

___

___

Embrace that a Loose Part Can Be Anything

Educators know how traditional toys in early childhood classrooms are to be used. Teachers have expectations, for example, that a truck is for driving, a puzzle is for putting together, and an astronaut costume is for blasting off into outer space. There is comfort in knowing how something should be played with. Early childhood training teaches us how to set up an environment, which types of materials to include in each play area, and how toys promote learning and development. So, when loose parts are added to

REFLECT

What preconceived notions of how children use materials do you have that may be getting in your way? What preconceived notions do you need to let go of?

____

____

____

____

____

____

____

____

an environment, educators may not be comfortable as they do not know how they should be used. Understand that we do not need to tell children how to use loose parts, and know there is no right or wrong way to play with them, provided children are not hurting themselves, others, or the materials. Their infinite possibilities offer a sense of freedom. A wood dowel can be used for stirring a concoction, drawing in the dirt, catching a fish, watching a bug to climb on it, or slaying dragons.

Let Go

Embracing loose parts play may mean that you need to let go of your ideas about how a child should play with a material. Not knowing how play is supposed to happen can be unsettling. It is not easy when things do not go the way we expect. For example, it was challenging to know how to react when I observed Ava picking up a stone. What was she going to do with it? What if she threw it? Instead of trying to control how she played with the stone, I stepped back and had faith in her ability. I trusted that it might not be what it seemed or what I feared. Ava surprised me as she began playing with the stone as a dinosaur egg. Letting go of what you deem correct material usage can mean more inventiveness and joy for children. Trust that eventually things will be okay.

Allow Time

Be aware that it may take time for you and children to transition to loose parts play. It has been my experience that the change is harder for educators than for children. Children thrive in loose parts environments, while some teachers have difficulty with change. Perhaps for adults it is the discomfort and uncertainty of stepping into the unknown. What are play and teaching supposed to look like in a loose parts environment? During the shift, your role as an

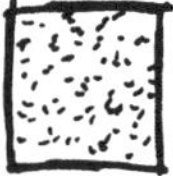

educator evolves, and there may be times of stress, confusion, and fear. You may feel disappointment or want to give up when things do not go perfectly. Doubt is a natural part of any adjustment period. Be assured that you and the children will feel more comfortable with time. Keep an open mind and be patient. It takes a long time to create a loose parts environment, and you should not rush it or expect to do it quickly. Hang in there—embracing a loose parts approach will have unbelievable rewards!

Use a New Lens

The word *teacher* implies that adults are to teach children—to offer instruction, demonstrate, and explain, and to tell children what to do and how to do it. This understanding of a teacher's role indicates that teachers are to *do something* to children. Know, however, that an early childhood educator's role is to facilitate rather than instruct. Educators who embrace a play-based philosophy watch and wait and recognize learning that happens while children play. They allow children to direct their own learning.

As adults, our childhood memories of school are often from when we were older in elementary school. Many adults in early childhood education programs teach as if they were an elementary school teacher, with a direct instruction approach. But good, developmentally appropriate teaching looks very different in early childhood. Early childhood education is different from the later years of school because young children are unlike older children, and they learn best through playing, exploring, and interacting with one another.

Embracing change requires that you keep an open mind. Rather than thinking of the outcome, enjoy the process. Focus on a growth mindset. Know that loose parts encourage purposeful movement and exploration, and view loose parts play as opportunity to expand children's development and learning.

REFLECT

How would you describe your teaching style? If your teaching style is mostly teacher directed, how can you shift your teaching style to be more facilitative or play based? What is challenging for you about switching to a more facilitative style?

____

____

____

____

____

____

____

CHAPTER 3

Getting Started

Taking stock of what loose parts you currently have is the first step in gaining an accurate assessment of your physical inventory and will help determine appropriate action for provisioning your program. It will help you know which play zones need loose parts as well as which loose parts to acquire. Involve children in the inventory process, as collecting data is part of the scientific inquiry process. Keeping a record of your loose parts journey will capture where you started and document how the changes you make affect children's play.

An inventory also helps detect "shrinkage" when the supply of certain loose parts is low or damaged and needs to be replaced. Putting a system in place for doing an inventory regularly helps you stay ahead of the replacement curve. Loose parts often "travel" or disappear. You may notice, for example, that the supply of small stones in the mud kitchen is down to just a few. Knowing when supply is dwindling will allow you to work on finding replacements. Here are some inventory tips:

- List locations of indoor and outdoor play zones and storage areas.
- Provide descriptions and/or take photos to identify and record the loose part types found in each play zone/storage area.

☐ **ACTION STEP**: Take an inventory of your current loose parts. Classify indoor and outdoor materials according to play zones (block, dramatic play, manipulative, and so forth). Take photos of the loose parts or jot them down below.

____

____

____

____

____

____

____

____

- Organize loose parts by placing like items together and discarding damaged pieces.
- Take a physical count of loose parts and record results.
- Review quantities and types of loose parts.
- Identify and list loose parts to add.

Determine Which Loose Parts to Add

After reviewing your current physical count, determine your inventory needs for each play zone.

- *Is a play zone lacking loose parts?* If loose parts are not present in a zone, consider what you could collect to add to or replace commercial toys. For example, add loose parts such as small bamboo segments, polished stones, and anise stars for creating designs in an art area. Replace plastic math manipulatives with natural loose parts such as shells and sea glass. If a play zone is sparse with loose parts, such as a sand area with only a few logs, add to the inventory.
- *Are some loose parts not working?* If children are not engaging with loose parts or they are using them inappropriately (such as throwing them), it is time for a change. Perhaps the loose part is not intriguing and substituting another type will help. For example, I have found that paper towel and toilet paper tubes are not exciting to children. Their light weight and thin cores make it difficult to build with them or balance them. Instead, children seem most intrigued with throwing or smashing them. Substitute these tubes with thick cardboard cores, which make stronger and more stable structures. Craft sticks alone are not appealing. Adding clothespins or shoestrings makes connecting and

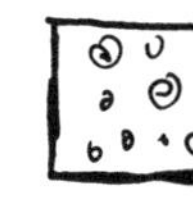

disconnecting possible. (See the frequently asked questions in chapter 7 for suggestions for handling inappropriate use of loose parts.)

- *Do some loose parts need replenishing?* Loose parts need replacing when damaged, broken, or soiled and when the quantity is too small for children to carry out their ideas.
- *Is it time to introduce a new loose part to the play area?* See the frequently asked questions in chapter 7 for advice on this.
- *Which loose parts may enhance play in the area?* Review appendices C and D for loose parts ideas.

Not sure where to begin? Start here.

Think Big

Some people equate the term *loose parts* with small things, but this is far from true. Many terrific loose parts are large. A successful path to implementing loose parts can start off by infusing big loose parts. Because they are big, they are not as overwhelming or messy as tons of tiny pieces. Your comfort level with loose parts will grow if you don't need to worry about different small items mixing, making a mess, and taking lots of time to clean up. Selecting large loose parts as children's first introduction to loose parts play will lower your stress level and pique children's interest.

Check out photos of large loose parts at this QR link or at www.redleafpress.org/lpa/largelp.pdf.

ACTION STEP: Make a list of large loose parts to acquire.

____

____

____

____

____

____

____

____

____

Here are a few of my favorite large loose parts:

- Cardboard boxes (sturdy)
- Cardboard yarn cones
- Carpet or hard-core cardboard tubes
- Cove molding
- Crates
- Gutters
- Plastic drinking cups (sturdy)
- Plastic spools for ribbon and wire
- Ramps
- Tin or paint cans
- Tree logs
- Wood or plastic cable reels
- Wood scraps

Think Flexibly

Undefined materials allow for maximum creativity. Simple items that do not have a lot of detail encourage the imagination. You can apply this same thinking for play furniture. Play is restricted to specific pretend cooking tasks in a dramatic play kitchen that contains a stove, sink, and refrigerator. If, however, these items are replaced with open shelving units, it allows countless play possibilities that may or may not be related to cooking. There's also more play space.

Check out these indoor and outdoor ideas at this QR link or in the appendix.

Think Indoor/Outdoor

Loose parts vary for inside and outside use depending on space and weather. Often outdoor spaces are larger than interior ones, which means that bigger loose parts can be used. Long wood planks, wood cable spools, and crates work well for constructing outdoors, while inside, shorter planks and tin cans are a better option.

Outdoor loose parts need to hold up to the elements. Inclines for trajectory may be gutters outdoors and cardboard cove molding inside. Balls may be rubber outdoors and felted wool inside. While items made of cardboard and fabric are not ideal outdoors during rainy and snowy seasons, they may work beautifully during warm seasons.

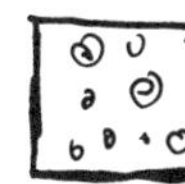

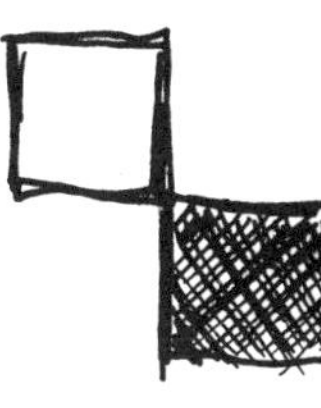

Add "Can't Miss" Loose Parts

It may be surprising to learn that open-ended materials are not created equal. Not all loose parts are captivating to children. Some are more alluring than others, and when they are placed in an environment, you can be assured of their success. Often these guaranteed-not-to-fail loose parts are simple, plain, nondescript items. I have observed thousands of children at play over the years, and through trying and testing loose parts, I have identified loose parts that have proven to be reliable and certain to have favorable results. This is not an exhaustive list by any means, as new loose parts continue to be discovered and children in your program may respond differently to specific ones, but I guarantee engagement with any of these loose parts.

Here is a list of "can't miss" loose parts:

- Bottle caps (plastic and metal)
- Buttons (large; 2" in diameter)
- Cinnamon sticks (at least 3 inches in length)
- Countertop tile samples (2" x 2"; smooth edges)
- Glass stones (large)
- Metal washers (large)
- Sea beans (1½"–2" in diameter)
- Self-grip hair rollers
- Stones
- Tin cans
- Tree cookies
- Wooden rings

Bottle Caps

Bottle caps of all shapes and sizes are easy to collect; asking for donations has the added benefit of encouraging family engagement. Every time we finish a container of milk at my house, I wash the cap and throw it in a container that I keep in a kitchen drawer. You will be amazed at the wide variety of colors and sizes of plastic jar lids, from the deep blue of mayonnaise jar lids to the bright orange of juice containers. I only keep plain caps without writing on them because I like a clean look. If families have a toddler at home, they may be a squeeze pouch family. Squeeze pouch caps come in a rainbow of colors and are wonderful for sorting, classifying, transporting, and designing. Pair with picture frames or place mats for design work. You can also purchase plastic caps from plastics corporations; they are less expensive when purchased in bulk.

Buttons

Large buttons (two inches in diameter) are a bit pricey but so fabulous. Jumbo coconut shell buttons come in bright colors such as purple, turquoise, and hot pink. They are an excellent first loose part to introduce because they are large, inviting, and engaging. Dramatic play is my favorite place to put them first where they'll become donuts, pancakes, eggs, and cookies. Pair with chenille stems for inserting opportunities. For younger children, add a wooden tissue box cover or a container with a slit cut in the lid for children to insert buttons into the top opening. Children may create sculptures with the buttons and playdough or clay or stack buttons to make tall towers. Add buttons to the water table along with scoops and tongs. Hide buttons in a sand table, and consider adding sieves to sift them out of the sand. Children may also sort, count, match, and group buttons.

Cinnamon Sticks

Cinnamon sticks add sensory appeal to children's play with their light reddish-brown color and wonderful aroma. In a mud kitchen, children may add them to their culinary creations; use them as a stirring stick; or pretend they are food such as bread, pepperoni, or cheese sticks. In a small imaginative play-scape, they may become logs. As an element for design and representational work, they are perfect for making arms, legs, sunrays, hair, or houses. They come in lengths of three inches or longer and may be purchased in bulk.

Countertop Tile Samples

There is nothing better than countertop tile samples for stacking, building, creating enclosures, matching, and pretending. Their smooth surface and rounded corners make them safe even for infants, and they have a fascinating magnetic quality when stacked on top of each other. My first introduction to tile samples came when I purchased a tile sample pack at a teacher's resource center. Now I purchase residential tile samples from manufacturers on the internet. Samples come in varying sizes and in extraordinary colors (the least expensive size is 2" x 2"). Make certain that samples have smooth, rounded corners, as some may have sharp sides and corners. Tiles last forever and are a great investment. Note that tiles are heavy, so consider the shipping costs before purchasing.

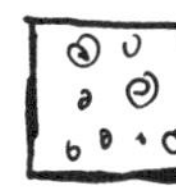

Glass Stones

Glass stones come in a wide variety of colors and sizes and are readily available at discount and craft stores. On a light table, glass stones invite children to explore color and light as well as create designs. Pair stones with clear shower curtain rings, plastic bracelets, colored acrylic sheets, or transparent colored drinking straws. Place colored stones on a light table in an acrylic or plastic container with compartments, such as a clear egg carton or divided serving tray. An invitation to play with glass stones on acrylic mirrors or metal trays lets children express their creativity. Provide an interesting piece of wallpaper with large circular swirls for children to place stones. Glass stones in the art area may become stunning designs in spirals and geometric shapes. Adding glass stones to dramatic play may yield unusual results. For example, in one early childhood program, Jessica pretended clear glass stones were soap bubbles as she washed dishes, and Kiela pretended they were poop in her baby's diaper.

Metal Washers

Large metal washers added to imaginary play may become money, food, or treasure. They make a wonderful sound when stirred or poured into a metal container. The shiny circular shapes are an intriguing enhancement to design work. For instance, one teacher observed Avril placing small metal washers on top of a canning lid to represent the design on a turtle's back. Washers may be counted and grouped according to size and type. Pair washers with a balancing or food scale for children to explore weight. Bury them in sand for children to dig up or use a colander or sieve to separate washers from sand. A music rod made with a threaded metal rod and washers brings unexpected delight to a sound garden. Children slide the washers to the top of the threaded rod and then let them go. As the washers cascade down, they sound like rain falling. Instructions for making a music rod are available on several internet sites. Ask family members to check home drawers, cabinets, and garages for extra washers (wash thoroughly before use). Take size into consideration if using with younger children. Washers are available for purchase at hardware stores and are less expensive when bought in bulk.

Sea Beans

Sea beans are large, smooth, mahogany-colored seeds from trees and vines that grow in tropical places and drift up on warm coastal beaches. These beans are one to two inches in diameter, which makes them a safe size for infants and toddlers. The versality of sea beans offers multiple possibilities: representing food in dramatic play; transporting; stacking; making designs and representations in art; patterning, counting, comparing, and measuring in math; feeling, burying, dunking, and exploring in sand and water areas; using as props in small world play. For example, Padma used sea beans to represent frogs as she retold a familiar story. Sea beans may be purchased commercially.

Self-Grip Hair Rollers

For children who are fascinated with connecting and disconnecting, you cannot go wrong with self-grip hair rollers. They are easy to manipulate, which makes them a great choice for children who are developing small-motor skills. Placed in a manipulative or construction area, children will spend hours constructing and deconstructing with them. Adding hair rollers to water or sand play results in intriguing investigations. Rollers in water float on top. Once submerged and released, they quickly spring up to the surface. Try pairing the rollers with a flannel board as a building surface. For children who are interested in trajectory, create a marble run on the flannel board by attaching curlers in an incline for marbles to roll down. Throwing rollers at the board also excites children who have a trajectory interest. It is a challenge to get the rollers to stick and a safe way to practice throwing. Self-grip rollers are good for inserting too. Pair the rollers with an accordion coffee mug holder (wood or metal), plastic crate with holes, or a paper towel holder for inserting. Self-grip rollers are available at a wide variety of discount stores and on the internet. Note: Always supervise and guide children's use of self-grip rollers as they can get tangled in hair.

Stones

Children find the weight, color, shape, and texture of stones captivating. Depending on their size, you can add stones to every indoor and outdoor play zone. Larger stones create opportunities for heavy work as children build curving roads, riverbeds, and dams in sand areas. Smaller stones work well for sorting, classifying, patterning, and counting as well as for design work. Stones

may be lined up, stacked, or transported. In imaginative play, children may use stones to represent candy in their candy store or potatoes in their soup. Stones provide opportunities for storytelling as they become props or take on names and personalities. A wonderful blend of maroons, grays, tans, charcoal, and ivory stones may be collected or purchased from landscaping and gardening centers. Painting stones with water brings out their beautiful natural colors.

Tin Cans

Tin cans are perfect for building, stacking, nesting, and lining. They are also good for sand, water, and mud kitchen play. Add them to indoor and outdoor block building areas. The crashing metal sound of falling cans is satisfying to young builders. Stack tins in a pyramid formation for tin can bowling. Knocking cans over will excite children interested in trajectory. The best part about tin cans is that they are free. Every educator needs a smooth-edged can opener in their tool kit. It opens cans with ease and leaves no sharp edge. Once opened, you have two loose parts—the can and the lid! Invite family members to collect tin cans in varying sizes. Send home a smooth-edged can opener for them to use. After opening cans, I always place them in the dishwasher for a good cleaning.

☐ **ACTION STEP**: Make a list of "can't miss" loose parts to obtain.

____

____

____

____

____

____

____

____

____

Tree Cookies

Every program needs massive quantities of tree cookies. Tree cookies—called cookies because their shape is round—are tree branches cut into slices like a loaf of bread. To make, cut slices of fallen branches from different types of trees in varying diameters gleaned from your yard, neighborhood, or nature hikes. (You can also purchase tree cookies on the internet.) Oak, cherry, walnut, camphor, aspen, poplar, ash, hickory, redwood, cedar, and birch each provide unique smells, color, texture, and weight. Be cautious with pine wood as it can be very sappy. If you are not handy or do not own a saw, solicit help from families

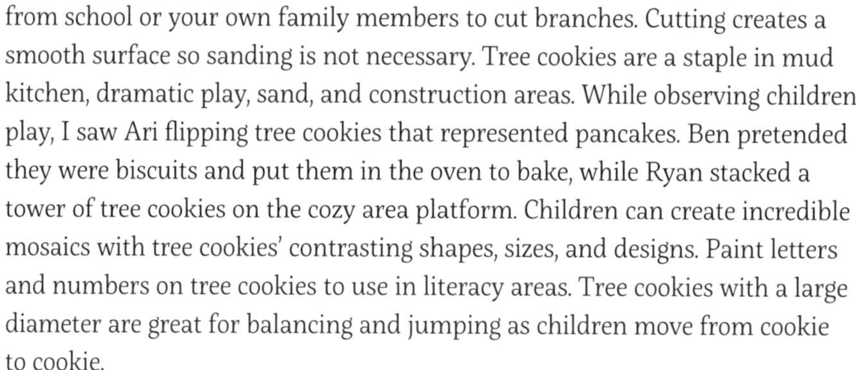

from school or your own family members to cut branches. Cutting creates a smooth surface so sanding is not necessary. Tree cookies are a staple in mud kitchen, dramatic play, sand, and construction areas. While observing children play, I saw Ari flipping tree cookies that represented pancakes. Ben pretended they were biscuits and put them in the oven to bake, while Ryan stacked a tower of tree cookies on the cozy area platform. Children can create incredible mosaics with tree cookies' contrasting shapes, sizes, and designs. Paint letters and numbers on tree cookies to use in literacy areas. Tree cookies with a large diameter are great for balancing and jumping as children move from cookie to cookie.

Wooden Rings

Wooden rings come in various sizes and are used for macramé, knitting, crochet, teething, and crafts. They are made from different woods, such as maple and beechwood. Their durability and smoothness make them an exceptional loose part that is appropriate for infants and toddlers. Many are designed as teething rings, so they are extra safe and easy to clean. Rings are available through online marketplaces and come in varying diameters, often given in millimeters. Be certain to ensure the size is large enough to be age appropriate. Rings are perfect for designing, manipulating, stacking, transporting, counting, matching, comparing, inserting, filling and dumping, and representing food.

Identify Resources

Scoring free loose parts is a bonus, but it may take a bit of detective work to uncover them. Free loose parts are found in a wide variety of places. Always use caution to ensure collected loose parts are safe for children. See the *Safety and Cleanliness* section on page 45 for more information. Check local laws if you wish to collect nature items in parks and public spaces.

Free loose parts can be found in a variety of places:

- Appliance stores: cardboard cove molding
- Backyards/neighborhoods: natural materials such as pine cones, rocks, leaves, seedpods
- Big-box retail stores: cardboard sheets, corrugated cardboard sheets, cardboard flats

- Family/friends/neighbors: Unexpected finds happen when you talk to family members, friends, and neighbors about loose parts. Once, a preschool family whose older children are involved in go-kart racing brought in a large supply of used go-kart tires (they are disposed of after every race). They are small and perfect for transporting, rolling, and constructing.
- Home accessory stores: cardboard rings placed in between glass bowls to prevent breakage
- Large businesses/schools: packaging material used to ship computers and monitors
- Online: The internet is full of giveaways if you know where to look. People post a variety of freebies on community websites and social media. Check out apps for free stuff in your neighborhood or near you. Some people want to find a home for unwanted things so they don't end up in a landfill. A few minutes of browsing may yield free tree stumps or other valuable finds. Use trustworthy sites and be cautious.
- Specialized businesses/factories: wood scraps, mat board, picture frame materials, wire, cable spools, plastics

☐ **ACTION STEP**: Make a list of local resources in your community where you can seek out free or inexpensive loose parts.

____

____

____

____

____

____

____

____

____

Where to find inexpensive loose parts:

- Consignment stores
- Discount variety stores
- Garage sales
- Restoration resource stores
- Teacher resource stores
- Thrift stores

Enlist Help and Involve Families

Astonishing results are possible when individuals get involved in collecting loose parts. Enthusiasm for finding loose parts is contagious, so be prepared. You will be amazed by how quickly loose parts multiply, more than you would imagine. Build your collection slowly by adding new loose parts each year, or add multiple types at a time.

Note: Sometimes well-intentioned individuals bring items that for a variety of reasons are inappropriate, but it may dampen their enthusiasm for helping if you reject their offerings (people are more willing to contribute when they know their effort is valued). For this reason, before beginning, consider which loose parts you want to collect and post a list.

Check out a family engagement letter at this QR link or in the appendix.

ACTION STEP: Make a list of individuals who can help collect loose parts. Consider people such as program families, personal family members, friends, and neighbors.

____

____

____

____

____

____

____

____

Since loose parts are often found, natural, and upcycled materials, inform family members about gathering only materials that are safe for children. For instance, smaller loose parts are a choking hazard for infants. Other loose parts may have associated risks, such as feathers that can carry disease or plants that are toxic. Additionally, caution families about gathering items where collection of natural materials is prohibited or illegal, such as state or national parks.

Learning about loose parts is a meaningful way to connect with families and involve family members in supporting their children's learning and development. Loose parts may be a new concept for families in your program, so you may need to introduce them. The hope is that as families learn about what loose parts are and their value, they will embrace loose parts play at home as well as at school.

Through my training experiences, I have found that family members vividly recall loose parts from their own childhood with immense joy. They remember using tin cans as balls to play kickball, sticks and rocks as baseball bats and

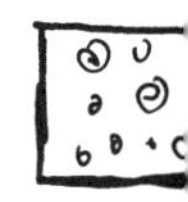

balls, found string to wrap things up, a tin cigar box to collect treasures, and a bent pot to make mud pies. Often family members are surprised and relieved to learn that they do not need to buy expensive toys to foster their child's learning; all that is needed for rich play can be found in their own home.

Loose parts are a shared experience. They invite conversation about past and present play experiences. Everyone has a loose parts story. I have yet to find anyone who has not played with a loose part as a child. Talking about these experiences fosters connection and intimacy between individuals.

Encourage children and family members to gather loose parts for collections in your program or their homes as they go about on family outings. You may end up with quite an assortment of rocks or pine cones. Soliciting family assistance in identifying and collecting loose parts helps families feel connected and valued. Collecting and finding loose parts helps children gain a sense of classroom ownership and community.

Quantity of Loose Parts

There is no magic formula for the number of loose parts to have in a program. The number depends partly on your comfort level; some educators can handle more loose parts than others. Know that an overabundance of loose parts can be overwhelming and cause children to become too active or excited. An insufficient number can frustrate children, limit play opportunities, and cause conflict. Having an ample source of loose

ACTION PLAN: FAMILY ENGAGEMENT

Develop a family engagement plan that includes the following:

- ☐ A letter introducing loose parts (see appendix A for a template)
- ☐ A list of needed loose parts that families may collect and some local places where they are likely to have good finds, such as their own homes, yards, and neighborhoods
- ☐ Ways for sharing childhood loose parts experiences
- ☐ Ways to implement loose parts at home
- ☐ ________________
- ☐ ________________
- ☐ ________________

Check out a family engagement letter at this QR link or in the appendix.

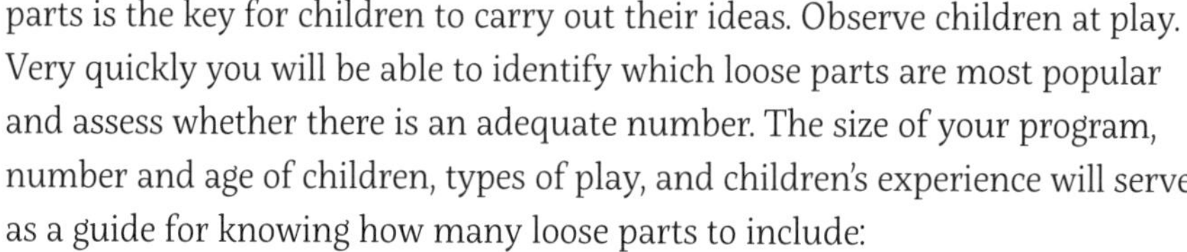

parts is the key for children to carry out their ideas. Observe children at play. Very quickly you will be able to identify which loose parts are most popular and assess whether there is an adequate number. The size of your program, number and age of children, types of play, and children's experience will serve as a guide for knowing how many loose parts to include:

- Program size: Larger programs have more square footage for play space and loose parts. Smaller programs have limited space and storage, which means they should have fewer loose parts to avoid having their space feel cramped or look chaotic and cluttered.
- Age: Infants are intrigued with the properties of materials and explore with their senses, so they need fewer loose parts. An infant may explore one smooth metal container by grasping or banging it. Toddlers may stack two or three tin cans on top of each other, whereas preschoolers may stack ten; thus, older children need three to four times the number of cans. Preschoolers require a lot of loose parts to carry out complex building plans.
- Number of children: Loose parts programs are play based and consist of large blocks of open-ended play. This means that all play centers are open at the same time and children are free to move about as desired. Not as many loose parts are needed when children control their play. For example, think about how your class might use plastic bottle caps in design and representational art. If these materials were part of a required group activity for eight children at the same time, you would need a massive number of bottle caps as children might become possessive and argue over inadequate materials. If, however, this is one of multiple flexible play options that children may self-select, fewer bottle caps are necessary.
- Type of play: How loose parts are used can affect the quantity needed. Consider design work. A child creating a simple design with natural materials may use ten pieces of sea glass, driftwood, and seashells, while a child creating an elaborate design on a whole tabletop may use fifty or more pieces. A child counting or sorting natural materials does not need a lot. Children placing plastic cups on a table and batting them off require just a few cups, whereas children who are building a complicated structure need many.

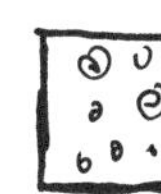

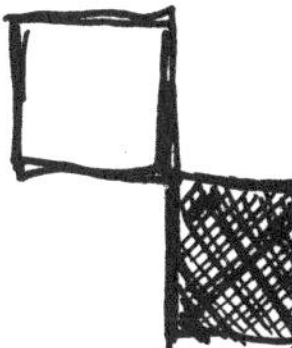

- Experience with loose parts: As children gain experience playing with loose parts, more are needed. Their prior knowledge influences how they use the materials. It becomes easier for children to generate new ways of using loose parts with each encounter. Constructions, design work, and imaginative play all increase in complexity as children's skills, abilities, and familiarity with loose parts increase.

Collection Phase

In the beginning, you will be gathering loose parts and must figure out how to organize them until there is an abundant supply of a given material you can add to the environment. Once you have collected a lot of loose parts, they will generally stay in the environment, unless you choose to store or rotate extra loose parts. Some outdoor loose parts may be placed in storage during inclement weather for protection.

Organizing collected loose parts may seem overwhelming at first. As loose parts come in, developing a collection system that works for you will make collection streamlined and efficient. A little extra work up front in setting up the system will mean less work overall.

Establish a centralized location for collecting loose parts. If you are requesting donations from families in your program, set up collection boxes in a courtyard, porch, center entrance, or welcome area. Place labeled baskets, containers, or bags outside of your program. People can place items they bring into the appropriate container. Label the containers according to material type, such as pine cones or jar lids. Begin with one or two designated boxes. After enough materials are collected, place them in the environment. Let families know when you have enough of a particular item. Relabel the collection boxes and begin accumulating the next desired loose parts.

Long-Term Storage

You may sometimes need long-term storage for the loose parts in your classroom. For example, continually adding loose parts may result in a crowded classroom. An educator may opt for permanent storage solutions rather than removing loose parts to make room for newly acquired items. At other times,

an educator may decide to store specific loose parts when not in use, such as items related to geographic locations or seasons. Seashells, sea glass, and driftwood may be stored and replaced with pond rocks, dirt, moss, and tree branches. The acorns, leaves, and gourds of autumn may be put away and replaced with wintery loose parts of pine boughs and cones. Below are useful tips for permanent storage options.

- *Invest in storage boxes or totes.* Have a container for each category or type of loose part. The container size will depend on the amount of storage space available as well as the size and quantity of loose parts. Storage bins with lids allow totes to be stacked and provide protection when stored in a garage or shed. Clear bins allow you to see what is inside and make things look more uniform. Purchasing the same brand means that lids always fit and that you don't waste time trying to figure out which lid fits which container. Consider using separate smaller bins or sealed plastic bags to organize materials such as postcards, business cards, and envelopes.
- *Determine your loose parts categories and label your containers.* Consider starting out using the common, broad categories below. Each loose part type may be placed in its own bag or container inside a larger category tote. For example, a natural materials tote may contain separated bags of pine cones, acorns, seedpods, sweet gum balls, and tree cookies. Over time you may find that some classifications work for you and others do not. For example, your natural materials may need two totes and paper or glass none.

ACTION PLAN: LOOSE PARTS COLLECTION

Develop a family engagement plan that includes the following:

- [ ] Determine location of centralized collection of loose parts and set it up with labeled containers.
- [ ] Notify family members about which loose parts to collect.
- [ ] Inform family members when enough of a particular loose part has been gathered.

ACTION PLAN: LOOSE PARTS STORAGE (IF DESIRED)

- [ ] Establish storage space.
- [ ] Obtain storage totes.
- [ ] Label totes obtained with selected categories.

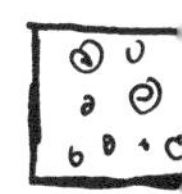

Here are some loose parts categories:

- Cardboard
- Fabrics and textiles
- Glass
- Metal
- Natural materials
- Paper
- Plastic and silicon
- Wood

Organize the bins in your storage area. Place totes used a lot at your waist or eye level so they are easy to find and retrieve. Arrange heavier totes on bottom shelves and rarely used loose parts on top or hard-to-reach shelves.

Helpful Storage Facts

Loose parts are not massive quantities. Since the term *loose parts* contains the word *loose* and is plural, it may conjure up an image of tons of materials. Perhaps you visualize an immense inventory of storage totes filled with loads of loose parts or classroom shelves overflowing with materials, but this is not reality. Rather, once enough loose parts are obtained, they are displayed in the environment, and auxiliary storage is not necessary. Loose parts on classroom shelves are organized in an inviting and aesthetically pleasing way that encourages children's exploration. The right quantity of loose parts is provided to allow choice, avoid clutter, and reduce disputes.

Less storage space is needed with loose parts than with traditional materials. Loose parts are kept available in the classroom or play yard and generally do not need to be stored. Early childhood educators are known for their ability to collect and save all kinds of materials that may be used one day for collages, sculptures, seasons, holidays, and science experiences. I know; I was one of those. These materials were not used as loose parts but as consumable materials for activities and experiences determined by me. I also kept large prop boxes for dramatic play themes, such as restaurant, firefighter, police officer, flower shop, and camping play, to name a few. These boxes were bulky and took up a lot of storage space. Twice a year—when items started falling off shelves and I could no longer close the storage shed door, get into the closet, or find what I was looking for—everything came out of storage for me to purge, discard, and reorganize. Perhaps you can relate to this situation. The good thing is that you don't need all these stored items with loose parts.

Loose parts are sustainable. Loose parts are used over and over, which eliminates the need to store extra supplies of consumable items. For example, in a conventional art area, collage work involves gluing various materials to a flat surface. Since items are permanently secured, they are not reusable and must be continually replenished. Boxes of collage materials are necessary. However, loose parts used for design or representational art are placed on a flat surface without glue. When finished, a photo may be taken if desired, and items are placed back in containers for use next time. There is no need to stockpile materials.

Loose parts remain in the environment, and rotating materials is generally unnecessary. Loose parts are always available and accessible in classrooms and play yards rather than in storage. Rotation is not necessary because of the affordances and variables inherent in loose parts. They are intriguing materials of which children do not tire. Play possibilities are endless with loose parts because of their open-ended nature. Since a loose part is unrestrictive and may be anything, children decide their intent, including using loose parts as dramatic play props. Children use their imaginations along with loose parts to create firefighter or fairy play. Additionally, because loose parts are developmentally inclusive, they are not above a child's developmental level. Thus, it is not necessary to have materials that satisfy different ages or abilities or rotate materials for more complex ones. Most loose parts are not centered around specific seasons, themes, or topics, so they are always suitable for any time of year. The flexibility of loose parts encourages creativity while limiting the need to store and rotate them.

If children are not engaging with specific loose parts, consider why not. Perhaps items need to be more visible, in a different play space, paired with an appropriate accessory, or displayed with visual appeal. Think about changes you could

☐ **ACTION STEP**: Place a sticky note on every container of loose parts with which children regularly engage. Keep these loose parts in the environment. For loose parts without sticky notes, consider changes to increase children's interest.

____

____

____

____

____

____

____

____

make to increase interest. The best loose parts storage options involve accessible display of items right in or near classroom and play yard learning spaces. Effective storage provides neatness and organization while helping children acquire a sense of independence and responsibility for accessing and putting away materials. (See more about storing loose parts within the environment in chapter 4.)

Mindful Retaining, Storing, and Discarding of Loose Parts

Individuals who are passionate about loose parts may argue that there can never be too many of them, but the reality is, at some point the quantity can become overwhelming. Just like shopping and buying clothes or shoes, how do you know when enough is enough? Is there a reasonable amount of loose parts to keep, and how do you decide what stays and what goes?

Space is limited at most centers and homes, and there is room for a finite amount of loose parts before clutter takes over, whether in the storage area or in the environment. As with other collections and materials, loose parts can quickly get out of control. Choices need to be made about keeping, storing, and letting go of loose parts. Below are suggestions to help.

To retain and store loose parts mindfully:

- Keep tried-and-true loose parts that children use regularly.
- Hang on to hard-to-obtain loose parts, such as coconut shells and film canisters. These materials will vary according to your geographic location and other circumstances.
- Keep or collect only what you have room to store. If space is limited, replace unused loose parts with new ones.
- Retain sturdier loose parts that hold up well over time, such as smooth tile samples.
- Keep multiples of the same loose part or a collection of similar ones, as more can be done with duplicates of the same item. Hoarding and sharing challenges are reduced when there are multiples.
- Get rid of random individual loose parts. A collection of pine cones is better than a few pine cones, a few seedpods, and a few acorns.

- Retain a variety of loose parts that offer different features, such as texture, weight, and color. For instance, keep loose parts that are natural, metal, and cardboard, not just all natural ones.
- Remove or rotate loose parts not being used by children. If loose parts have not been used in the past month, try moving them to a new location, displaying them differently, or adding a different material alongside them. If they are still unused after these changes, it may be time to remove them from the environment to reintroduce later or let them go.
- Save loose parts that you love or are sentimental to you, such as stones collected with Grandma on a special trip to the river. There are some loose parts that just bring joy. For me, these are natural items rich in colors and textures.

To dispose of loose parts mindfully:

- Clear out damaged or worn-out loose parts.
- Clear out similar loose parts if there is an overabundance. For instance, comparing is an essential math skill, but it is not necessary for children to have tons of materials to sort, classify, count, and make patterns. One divided container full of shells or bottle caps is sufficient.
- Eliminate loose parts that are easy to find or obtain if you have too many to store. They can be replaced easily when needed. This might include materials such as leaves or plastic bottle caps.
- Discard loose parts that have outlived their time on a storage shelf. I have containers of what I thought were neat loose parts on garage shelves to introduce to children one day. Be realistic. If that one day has not come in the past year, it's time to let go.
- Discard or donate loose parts that you or children no longer like or find interesting. Give away loose parts that you thought children would love but do not get much attention.

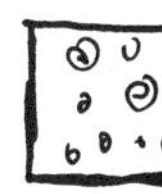

Safety and Cleanliness

Children's safety is always top priority in every early childhood program. Play with loose parts is not exceedingly risky, although there are a few potential possibilities associated with loose parts play to consider before placing them into the environment. Know that nothing will reduce potential accidents more than regular inspection of loose parts and active, responsive supervision of children at play. Since loose parts are often found and upcycled materials, special caution is necessary to ensure they are safe for children. Loose parts that get used a lot need to be sturdy or regularly replaced. Most loose parts are washable, but others, such as cardboard, are not. Below are some safety guidelines for selecting and maintaining loose parts.

Choking. Choking is probably the number one safety concern with loose parts, particularly for infants. Here are some tips to decrease choking risks:

- Consider size. Make certain loose parts are large enough for younger children by using a choke test cylinder to check size. Items that fit inside the cylinder are too small for infants and toddlers to use.
- Make sure loose parts do not have small pieces that might break off from a larger piece.
- Only allow children to use very small loose parts under active adult supervision, with focused attention and intentional observation of children.
- Ensure items may be safely used for mouthing. Be mindful of any children who have a condition such as autism or whom you have observed frequently putting items in their mouths.

Throwing and hitting. Throwing loose parts or using them to hit may be intentional or unintentional. Regardless of the reason, hard loose parts such as stones can cause damage if they hit someone or something. Here are some tips to decrease throwing and hitting risks:

- Anticipate throwing and hitting behavior. Use your knowledge of the children to predict what they might do, and stay close.
- Do not overreact and immediately remove hard materials. Instead, review classroom guidelines with children for handling hard materials.

For example, rocks are for carrying and wood scraps are for building. Trust in children's ability to alter their behavior and monitor them closely as they learn the right way to handle materials.

- Talk with children who accidentally hit another child. Explain results of their actions. Have the child who did the hitting participate in first aid for the child they hit, such as holding an ice pack on the hurt body area.
- Determine whether a child is exploring a trajectory schema. If you believe that to be the case, set up trajectory opportunities to satisfy the child's desire to explore items moving in space. This can include a target for throwing items at. Throwing a ball at a tower of tin cans or cardboard tubes set up as bowling pins are good options.
  - If throwing hard objects does not decrease, consider providing softer loose parts such as felted balls and loofahs for children to throw off a play loft or into a large container.

REFLECT

What safety concerns do you have about loose parts play? What actions can you take to lessen your concerns?

____

____

____

____

____

____

____

____

Falling from child-built structures. Large loose parts such as tires, wood crates, and wood planks are versatile items for children to build outdoor obstacle courses and low climbing structures with countless climbing, balancing, and jumping opportunities. Here are some suggestions for ensuring children's safety:

- Make certain that large loose parts are sturdy.
- Allow building on a ground surface designed to provide protection in the event of a child's fall.
- Double-check child-made climbing structures to guarantee stability.

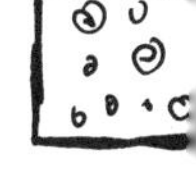

ACTION PLAN:

ENSURING SAFE PLAY WITH LOOSE PARTS

Consider the following items for assessing and addressing safety and hazards:

- Provide yourself and other educators with safety training on handling issues related to loose parts play to prevent injuries and ensure children are always kept safe. This may include identifying loose parts hazards, assessing factors contributing to risk of injury, and determining how to reduce risks.
- Outline expectations and responsibilities for educators who share the task of facilitating loose parts play. For instance, who is responsible for checking the condition of loose parts in the environment, and how often is this done? What is the role of educators to ensure safety while children are engaged in loose parts play?
- Define expectations and responsibilities for children's use of loose parts. For instance, involve children in developing guidelines about using loose parts safely.
- Create procedures for accepting loose parts, including donation requirements such as size and types of materials. Set up a system for checking the safety of newly acquired loose parts.
- Define how loose parts will be inspected for hazards.
- Establish processes for identifying, removing, and mitigating loose parts that have become hazardous.

- Give children space and freedom to gradually increase their competencies.

- Offer a question for consideration. "I wonder what might happen when you step on that wobbly plank?" or "What might you do differently to make the plank stabler?"
- Provide a direct comment. "I'm worried that plank may slip off the tire when you step on it."
- Suggest another option. "What do you suppose will happen if you placed the plank's end in the middle of the tire instead of on the tire's edge?" or "What might happen if you used one tire instead of stacking one on top of the other?"

Before placing loose parts into the environment, inspect them to make sure they are free from these things:

- Broken pieces
- Dirt
- Insects
- Mold
- Sharp edges
- Splinters

Follow these cleanliness recommendations for loose parts:

- Clean and disinfect frequently used loose parts regularly (such as stones, seashells, plastic caps), following state or licensing recommended protocols to prevent the spread of disease.
- Toss or compost when broken into pieces (such as leaves or tree cookies).
- Brush off dirt (such as acorns or sticks).
- Throw out if wet if the item is damaged or could grow mold.
- Replace and replenish as needed.

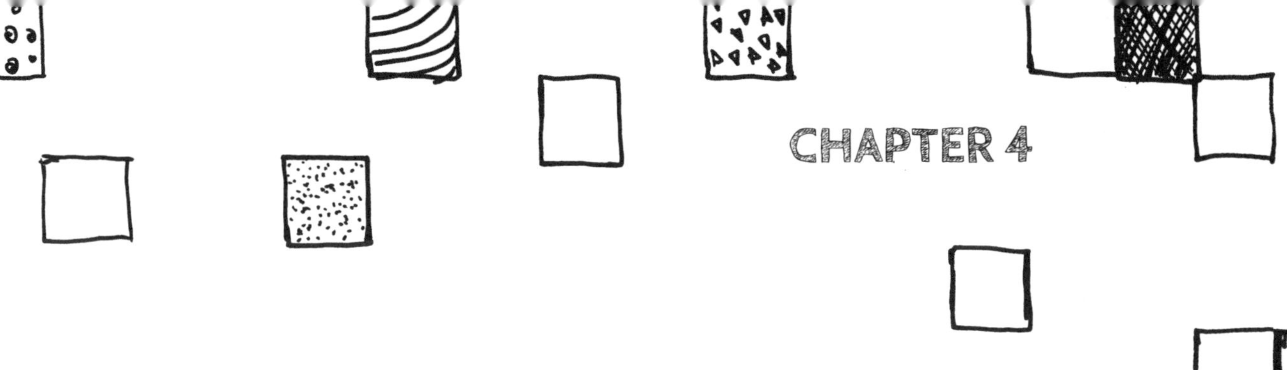

CHAPTER 4

Preparing the Enviroment

Infusing loose parts into your environment may seem to be a tremendous task. At times educators see beautiful "after" photos of loose parts environment transformations and question how they can ever achieve it. That's where this manual comes in; it's designed to help you whether you want to introduce just a few loose parts into your program or transform your whole environment into a loose parts classroom. Through a series of steps, you'll learn how to set up appealing environments and promote meaningful play successfully and effectively using loose parts. With each action you take, you will change children's engagement and enrich their learning. I recommend starting small and taking steps one at a time according to your own comfort level.

Here are some tips:

Be patient with the process. We often want our classroom to be fabulous immediately. Remember it takes time to create a rich environment. The best early childhood environments are continually evolving and changing according to children's interests, abilities, and needs. Teachers have an intrinsic passion for discovering new materials and experiences. They delight in learning creative and inspirational ideas and can't wait to implement them in the classroom and see children's engagement. Know that everything does not need to be done right

REFLECT

Describe your current feelings about implementing loose parts into your program. What are you excited or apprehensive about?

____

____

____

____

____

____

____

____

away. Take time and gradually add interesting finds from weekend expeditions and garage sales.

You don't need to do it alone. Going through the process is much easier with reflective colleagues who have shared goals. Coworkers or a group of fellow educators can provide you with encouragement, comfort, and advice, as well as opportunities to share experiences and feelings, bounce around ideas, brainstorm obstacles, and problem solve. Solicit guidance, advice, and feedback from a mentor, someone who has been through the process and can share knowledge and wisdom about infusing loose parts into environments.

It's okay to take a break. Stepping away from the transformation work can give you renewed energy and a new perspective. Taking the opportunity to recharge is especially important if you are feeling overwhelmed. Focus on one step at a time. Don't rush things; take it slow and steady. The transformation task will become more manageable with time. Make one change in the environment. Observe how children use the loose parts. Reflect, evaluate, and plan the next step.

Clear the Way

Begin the process of infusing loose parts into your environment by decluttering and organizing the learning spaces.

The organization process will help you do the following:

- Feel in control
- Think more clearly
- Let go of things
- Identify what is important to keep
- Create an efficient, well-organized environment for children and educators
- Create a predictable environment that provides a sense of stability and calm
- Promote success for children

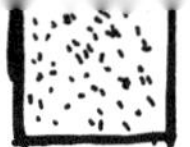

Some educators have a misconception that loose parts environments are messy and filled with a lot of stuff. This is far from the truth. Loose parts environments are simple and thoughtful. Their simplicity brings harmony and calmness. When an environment is simple, children's attention focuses on what is important: captivating materials for play. Effective classrooms with loose parts are clutter free. Think "less is more." Simplifying starts with getting rid of things that are not needed, particularly items that serve little play value.

Here are simple organizational steps to follow:

- Focus on one space: Looking at your entire environment can be overwhelming, so choose one play area or space at a time.
- Remove everything: Clear off all surfaces and clean thoroughly. Remove any tape and contact paper residue as well as marker and crayon scribbles.
- Put away: Return any items that are in the wrong place back to their intended spaces.
- Trash: Throw away or recycle items that are not worthy of being kept, such as nonrepairable toys or old magazines that are falling apart.
- Donate: Set aside items to pass on. Consider materials the children no longer play with or materials that will be replaced with loose parts. A small program space may compel you to really pare down the number of materials. When you do not have a lot of space to work with, keep a minimum number of materials. Since loose parts are multipurpose, it is not necessary to have as many.
- Repair: Set aside items to fix or mend. Place them alongside a "Fix Me" sign in the family welcome area. Family members may be delighted to mend books or restitch a seam on a cape.

☐ **ACTION STEP**: List colleagues, friends, and mentors who might provide ongoing support.

____

____

____

____

____

____

____

____

____

- Determine what to keep: Carefully think about which materials to keep. The contents contribute to the feeling of the room. Artificial materials may feel cold, while materials made of natural textures generate a sense of warmth and beauty. Think about how you feel when surrounded by nature. Peaceful? Calm? Happy? Creative?

ACTION PLAN: ORGANIZE A SPACE

- ☐ Space to transform:

  ____

- ☐ Remove everything
- ☐ Put away items
- ☐ Trash
- ☐ Donate
- ☐ Repair
- ☐ Determine what to keep

Exchange Materials

Identify items in the learning center to exchange for authentic pieces and loose parts. For example, in the dramatic play area, replace plastic cookware, pots, and pans with real cookware and utensils, and in the water area, replace plastic containers with real measuring cups. Exchange plastic food for maple rings, glass stones, or large metal washers. Let the process guide you, and observe the effects of your changes. After adding real cooking utensils and loose parts in the dramatic play area, one educator watched children's frustration grow as the remaining play cookware pieces were small and the new authentic utensils were large, making it hard for children to stir and mix loose parts. Her next action step became searching for adult-sized pots and pans.

Science Before

Science After

Select Containers

Now that you have identified the best materials and loose parts to keep, it's time to select containers. Here are characteristics to consider:

- Natural: Baskets offer functional beauty as well as a warm natural touch to a classroom. Their neutral color coordinates well with all color palettes. Consider quality and durability when selecting baskets.
- Solid color: Solid color or clear containers allow materials to be highlighted and attract children's attention. Materials get lost in multicolored containers. Additionally, avoid brightly colored containers that can overstimulate children or draw the eye away from the contents.
- Shallow: The depth of a container is important. Shallow containers allow for contents to be visible. Children can easily see what is available and do not have to rummage through or dump out materials to find what they need. One of my favorite storage baskets are wicker napkin holders.
- Uniform: Uniformity with color, material, or shape and size gives a classroom cohesiveness. Having uniform shapes, sizes, and colors of containers in the classroom is appealing.
- Compartments: Containers with compartments keep materials organized together, save space, and help organize smaller items. Loose parts may be arranged in container sections according to various qualities, such as size, shape, color, or material. A divided storage container has an open design that keeps items visible, allows easy access for children to reach materials, and permits children to easily carry materials to their preferred workspace. Sectioned containers also imply that the loose parts are special. Children are more likely to handle them with reverence and care.
- Handles: Caddies or baskets with built-in handles make it easy for children to transport loose parts from shelf to work surface and prevent items from falling out while being carried. Open tops make it easy for children to see what is inside and take what they need.
- Unusual: Uncommon containers provide intrigue in addition to function. For example, a handmade ceramic toothbrush holder may be

ACTION PLAN:
LIST LOOSE PARTS

- [ ] List authentic materials that can replace toys or pretend items in the learning center.

____

____

____

____

- [ ] List loose parts you currently have that can replace toys or pretend items in the learning center.

____

____

____

____

- [ ] List loose parts and authentic materials that you can collect to support and encourage play in the learning center.

____

____

____

____

perfect for holding easel brushes. A gourd with its top cut off may serve as a container for individual sand play.

Divided or sectioned container ideas

- Caddies
- Cosmetic organizer trays
- Food compartment trays
- Jewelry storage containers
- Lazy Susans
- Muffin tins
- Nut and bolt organizer
- Ornament box
- PVC pipe sections
- Sectioned trays (wood, metal, plastic, wicker)
- Silverware drawer organizer
- Soda crate
- Vegetable divider tray

Mounted storage ideas

- Baskets or buckets hanging on a fence
- Bin organizers
- Coffee mug rack (wall mounted)
- Floating shelves
- Fruit basket
- Pocket shoe organizers
- Slanted shelving
- Spice rack organizer
- Wall-mounted organizer
- Wood crates

Furniture storage ideas

- Bench
- Coffee table with underneath shelf
- Cube storage organizer or bookcase on side
- Rolling storage cart
- Shoe racks

Display Loose Parts

How loose parts are presented in an environment is just as important as the type of loose parts selected. Their placement will influence the way they are handled. When something is accessible, visually appealing, and intriguing, it automatically captures our attention. Think of shopping at a store where you can easily see what's available and the clothing is attractively displayed on racks. Compare that image to a store where items are piled high and you need to weed through the inventory to see what there is. How items are staged affects our response and ability to process. This same concept is true when presenting loose parts. Children are apt to avoid loose parts they cannot see or reach or treat them inappropriately if they are visually overstimulating. On the other hand, children notice when loose parts are aesthetically displayed and inviting. It is hard for a child to walk past something that encourages investigation, provokes action, and stimulates thinking.

Consider the following basic principles when displaying loose parts:

- Accessibility and visibility: Accessibility means being able to easily get or use an item. Loose parts need to be within children's reach. Children should be able to approach materials freely without physical restriction. Accessibility also involves being able to independently remove materials and return them to the shelf. Containers that are too heavy can be a challenge for children to handle and can even present a safety concern. Consider the weight of items in containers and put heavier items on lower shelves. Visibility means easily seen, so children can discover, identify, and engage with loose parts. Items need to be easily approachable, visible, and conveniently stored on low open shelves for effective use.
- Close to intended use: Store items as close to their related use as possible. This is the same concept used in your home, such as when

☐ **ACTION STEP**: Identify containers and unique options for storing loose parts within play spaces.

____

____

____

____

____

____

____

____

ACTION PLAN:
EXCHANGE MATERIALS AND DISPLAY LOOSE PARTS

Play space where I will add loose parts: ____________________

- ☐ Take a before photo.
- ☐ Clear the way.
- ☐ Following the action steps on page 52, exchange materials for authentic items and loose parts.
- ☐ Select and collect or purchase containers.
- ☐ Display loose parts following basic display principles.
- ☐ Take an after photo.

dishes, glasses, and silverware are stored in cabinets close to the sink or dishwasher to make putting them away easier. In your classroom environment, place items so they are within children's reach, near where they will be used. Store hand tools like tongs in a container next to a pot and bowl of shoelaces in the dramatic play area. This way children have everything they need for making spaghetti and do not have to walk across the room to get something when they are in the middle of play. Display materials right on work surfaces or on nearby shelving units, counters, or window ledges. Some sensory and light tables have shelves mounted underneath that are perfect for storing accessories.

- Functionality: While loose parts are open-ended and have infinite possibilities, how and where they are displayed can determine the ways children engage with them. Their purpose or range of functions can vary. Depending on where loose parts are placed, they may be used for such actions as designing, imagining, building, creating, transforming, and investigating. Consider what might happen when you add wooden rings to your environment. What they are paired with gives an unstated clue about what to do with the loose parts.

Check out photos of loose parts displayed in classroom environments at this QR link or at www.redleafpress.org/lpa/iaolp.pdf.

Displaying Loose Parts

Wooden Rings Paired with:	*Encourages:*
Paper towel holder	Inserting rings on dowel
Muffin tin	Counting, sorting
Bowl and spoon	Stirring, scooping
Bucket	Transporting, filling, dumping
Place mat	Designing, placing
Sensory table with sand	Burying, sifting

CHAPTER 5

Introducing Loose Parts

Both educators and children encounter a learning period when loose parts are introduced into a play environment. Most often the challenges are greater for educators than for children. As one director stated, "The children seemed to instinctively know how to play with loose parts while educators questioned appropriateness. Is it okay for them to take the loose parts to another area? Can they do that with the loose part? Is that safe? Are they supposed to . . . ?"

Anticipate the Excitement Factor

New materials placed into an environment create excitement, which is a good result, as demonstrating curiosity and enthusiasm for materials and experiences is key to creativity and innovation. However, when many children gravitate to new additions, there may not be enough materials for everyone to successfully participate. Negative behaviors such as crowding, pushing, grabbing, or complaining may be unwelcome results, as preschool teacher Andrew discovered. Andrew got new tires on his car and couldn't wait to bring the old ones to school as the children's first loose part on the play yard. As he predicted, the children's curiosity and enthusiasm were immense. Unfortunately,

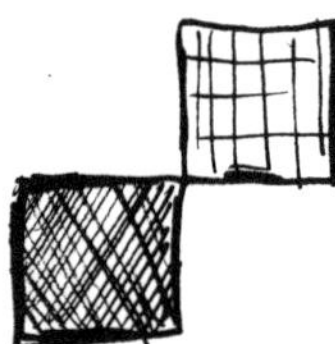

the interest was so great that conflict arose as so many children wanted to play with them.

Plan before leaping. While tires are a great loose part, Andrew needed to plan ahead. Four tires are not enough for a class of sixteen children, particularly if there are no other captivating play options in the yard. Adding more tires or combining tires with wood planks, crates, and wood cable spools would enhance the play and welcome multiple children to participate. Quantity is important for large-scale construction. Adding more tires or waiting to add tires to the play yard until after other large loose parts were gathered would have resulted in a more successful outcome.

REFLECT

What excites, worries, or concerns you about introducing loose parts?

____

____

____

____

____

____

____

____

Introduce One Loose Part at a Time

Start small and add loose parts little by little, particularly if you are easily overwhelmed. This means once you have acquired enough of one kind of loose part, introduce it into the environment. For example, add a bowl of wooden rings to the dramatic play area. After children are familiar with the rings, add another type of loose part. At the beginning of a school year, an early childhood classroom consists of minimum materials. Throughout the year, as children's familiarity and competency increases or interests change, educators add a variety of new materials. The same philosophy applies to loose parts. It is easier to add and grow loose parts slowly rather than overfill a classroom at first and regret the results.

Select a play area and a loose part. Consider one play area in the learning environment and a "can't miss" loose part to introduce. Be certain to collect enough of the loose part to facilitate positive play before placing it in the environment. Place loose parts in a space you feel will lead to children readily encountering them. Dramatic play, block, and sensory areas (water, sand, playdough, clay) are good choices as these spaces are easily suited to loose parts.

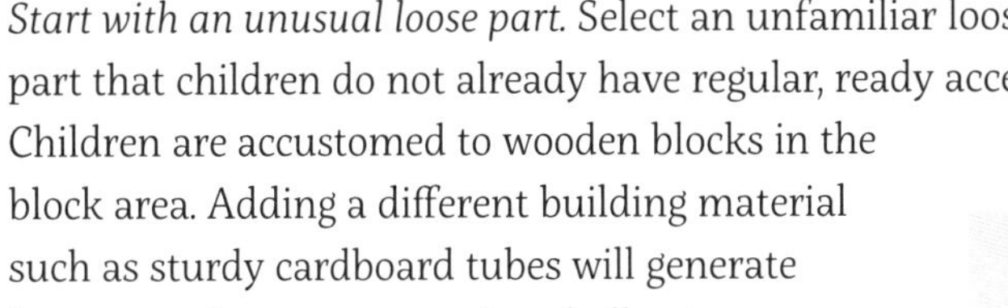

Start with an unusual loose part. Select an unfamiliar loose part. A loose part that children do not already have regular, ready access to is captivating. Children are accustomed to wooden blocks in the block area. Adding a different building material such as sturdy cardboard tubes will generate interest and new construction challenges.

Start with Bigger, Durable Loose Parts

Sturdy loose parts that are on the large side are a good option when first introducing loose parts. With larger loose parts, you will not be concerned about breakage or heavy use or be overwhelmed by the sheer number of smaller loose parts. Strong cardboard tubes, large plastic bottle caps or metal lids, sizable tree cookies, or tree blocks are good considerations. Once children use these loose parts safely and carefully, smaller, fragile loose parts such as glass stones may be added.

Avoid tiny materials. Be thoughtful in your selection of loose parts. I once observed a practicum student add a huge quantity of tiny beads and pom-poms to the dramatic play area. Her thinking was that children could fill, pour, and mix the items and pretend they represented a variety of food. The intent was good; however, beads and pom-poms mixed and went everywhere, and it took forever to clean up all the pieces. Loose parts should be large enough to easily pick up if spilled.

Do not use real food as a loose part. Food items such as dry beans, peas, lentils, pasta, or rice are not loose parts and are not appropriate to add into an environment. It may seem innocent to use such food for sensory or dramatic play, but many families are facing food insecurity. Food used for play could be a meal for a family. Additionally, we do not want to send children a message that playing with food is okay.

REFLECT

Are you a leaper or are you cautious when it comes to new experiences? What steps will help you successfully approach the implementation of loose parts?

Check out photos of large loose parts at this QR link or at www.redleafpress.org/lpa/largelp.pdf.

Check out appendix C for additional indoor loose parts at this QR link or in the appendix.

Best Loose Parts to Start: Indoors

Learning Center	*Loose Parts to Add*
Block	Plastic cups, sturdy cardboard tubes, planks of wood, tin cans, cardboard cove molding, felted balls
Dramatic Play	Scarves, sea beans, tree cookies, wood checkers, wooden rings, large buttons, large metal washers
Manipulative	Self-gripping hair rollers, plastic bottle caps and muffin tins, nesting cups, wooden spools
Sensory	Abalone, scallop, and coconut shells; measuring cups; graduated cylinders; seashells

Check out appendix D for additional outdoor loose parts at this QR link or in the appendix.

Best Loose Parts to Start: Outdoors

Play Zone	*Loose Parts to Add*
Outdoor Kitchen	Pots, pans, metal and wooden spoons, tree cookies, stones, driftwood
Sand	Abalone, scallop, and coconut shells; stones; driftwood, metal buckets, and scoops
Water	Gutters, measuring cups, graduated cylinders, funnels, driftwood, seashells
Trajectory	Gutters, ramps, corrugated drainage pipe, balls
Sound Garden	Pots, pans, metal trash cans, wood and metal spoons and spatulas

☐ **ACTION STEP**: Select a play area and a loose part. Display the loose parts and observe children's reactions.

____

____

____

____

Observe Children's Engagement

Once you've added loose parts to the environment, step back and observe what happens. Breathe, relax, watch, and wait. Do not direct play or jump in quickly to stop play. If you have selected a tried-and-true loose part that is plentiful and correctly placed in the environment, all will be well. Teacher Sunitha was concerned about children taking dramatic play loose parts to other areas of the classroom. She watched as children gathered scarves, bowls, and metal rings. She decided just to watch rather than stop their play. The children created a picnic setting with the materials on the block area floor. When it was time to clean up, the children picked up the loose parts and returned them to their original location. Sunitha was glad she did not object to the children's plan as they were engaged for an extended time and their play was rich

REFLECT

As children engage with loose parts, what actions make you most uncomfortable or nervous? What is your typical response to such behavior?

____

____

____

____

____

____

____

____

REFLECT

Observe children's play with loose parts. What needs to be your next step based on the children's responses?

____

____

____

____

____

____

____

____

and meaningful. I often ask, "What is the worst thing that could happen?" Usually, it is a learning opportunity, such as asking for help to make carrying a heavy object easier or understanding the consequence of having to pick up loose parts on the floor. Trust that children are capable, competent, and terrific problem solvers.

Observe how children are engaging with the loose parts, and reflect to determine your next steps. Are they using the loose parts respectfully? What seems to be the intent of their play? Become a keen observer. How the children respond to the loose parts will determine your next steps.

If children are:

- Competing for loose parts: Increase quantity of loose parts or add variety (another type of loose part).
- Not noticing loose parts: Change locations. Try moving the loose parts to another location or putting them in several spots simultaneously. The right learning space can make a difference. Consider a tabletop, floor, shelf, or tray.
- Not engaging with loose parts: Teacher Sarah placed PVC pipes in the children's play yard and waited with eager anticipation to see their engagement. Unfortunately, the children did not engage with the materials. When this happens, revisit the display and reexamine how the loose parts are set up. Do the loose parts stand out? Are they visible in the container? Are they easily accessible? Are there the right accessories to accompany the loose parts? Not much can be done with lengths of PVC pipe except perhaps pretend they are swords. The simple addition of pipe fittings lets children change the end type of a pipe and connect pipes of many sizes to extend play possibilities. Are the

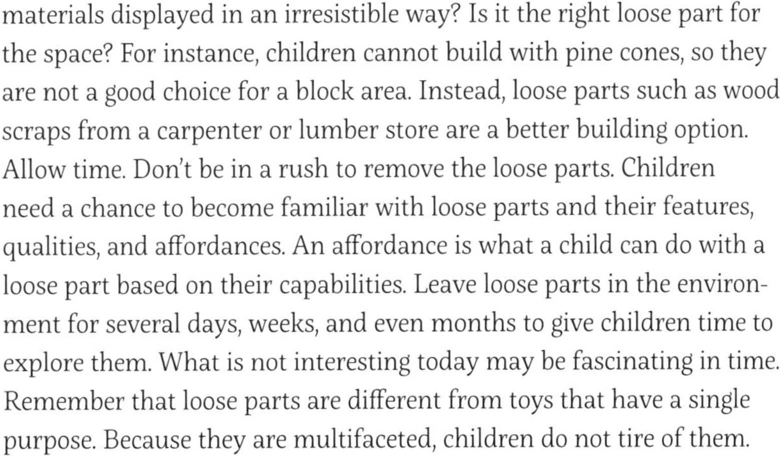

materials displayed in an irresistible way? Is it the right loose part for the space? For instance, children cannot build with pine cones, so they are not a good choice for a block area. Instead, loose parts such as wood scraps from a carpenter or lumber store are a better building option. Allow time. Don't be in a rush to remove the loose parts. Children need a chance to become familiar with loose parts and their features, qualities, and affordances. An affordance is what a child can do with a loose part based on their capabilities. Leave loose parts in the environment for several days, weeks, and even months to give children time to explore them. What is not interesting today may be fascinating in time. Remember that loose parts are different from toys that have a single purpose. Because they are multifaceted, children do not tire of them. I have witnessed building blocks going unused for quite a while, and then one day renewed interest happens and the block area is filled with eager builders.

- Actively using loose parts: Infuse loose parts throughout the environment. Add more loose parts (in quantity and in type) in other learning spaces and zones. Loose parts always need to be freely available for children throughout the classroom or play yard.

Prepare Children

When loose parts are properly infused into an environment, children automatically know what to do. Often a child is present as I am transforming a classroom or play yard. The child will immediately dive into a learning space and begin to play with the loose parts without direction. Some areas may require a little guidance, such as knowing how to get water in a mud kitchen, but for the most part, no instruction is needed. Play with loose parts is a universal language.

REFLECT

What is children's prior experience with loose parts? How do you predict they will respond to loose parts in your environment?

____

____

____

____

____

____

____

____

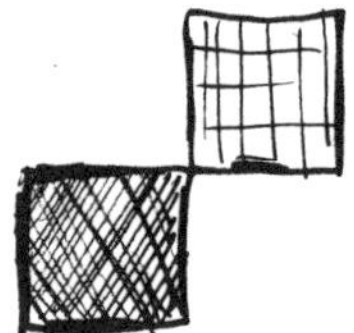

If the children in your class are not familiar with loose parts and you are concerned about their response, consider the following ways to introduce them.

Read a loose parts book. Read a children's book in which a character engages with a loose part. Hold a conversation about the many ways the character used the loose part in the book. Solicit ideas from children about how they might use a box, rock, or stick. Some children's book examples are:

Elizabeti's Doll by Stephanie Stuve-Bodeen (rock)

Galimoto by Karen Lynn Williams (wire)

Leaf Man by Lois Ehlert (leaves)

Not a Box by Antoinette Portis (box)

Not a Stick by Antoinette Portis (stick)

Roxaboxen by Alice McLerran (pebbles, stones, wooden boxes, pottery pieces, desert glass, stick)

Ruby's Sword by Jacqueline Veissid (stick)

Present loose parts at a group gathering. Showing a loose part and asking children to talk about its possibilities at a group gathering helps them become acquainted with it. Recall that you are soliciting children's ideas and not offering your ideas. Model handling the loose part slowly, carefully, and respectfully. Give each child a loose part such as a tree cookie or napkin ring to feel and explore. What do they notice about it? How does it feel? How could it be used? Remember that there is not a right or wrong way to use a loose part, so all ideas should be acknowledged. Talk about where in the environment the materials will be placed and solicit ideas about how they might be used. These initial invitations to play with loose parts will serve as a springboard to future provocations and explorations.

Set up an invitation. Offering a hands-on experience engages children's senses and imagination. Think of inviting ways to set up loose parts on an ongoing basis. Choose the learning space, loose parts, and accessories and stage the materials for engagement. For example, place small bowls of beautiful tiles next to a large ball of clay. Place colorful, transparent cups on the perimeter of the light table. Stack a few cups to serve as a prompt. Stage an attractive array of loose parts on a lazy Susan along with defined workspaces such as place mats. Place a few loose parts on the work surface with more off to the side. The idea is to offer a bit of a suggestion of what to do with the loose parts without overdoing it. A child may think, "Someone has already played here and there is nothing more for me to do," if there are too many things in place. A child may also walk past the loose parts if nothing is staged and they do not know what to do.

Point out loose parts usage. During gathering opportunities such as story, meal, and reflection times, talk about ways you have seen children use loose parts. "Today I saw Sam put wooden rings up to his eyes as if he were wearing eyeglasses. Gen put rings on her ears like earrings. Mikal was stirring and mixing the rings in a pot, and Nathan inserted a shoelace through rings and tied them together." Your comments will provide encouragement.

Use loose parts to tell a nursery rhyme or story. Tell a favorite nursery rhyme using loose parts. For example, "Humpty Dumpty" can be told with a tree cookie as Humpty Dumpty, a cardboard tube cut lengthwise as the wall, and small tree blocks as the king's horses and men. Leave the loose parts in the environment for children to tell the rhyme.

Solicit children's ideas. Raise questions about what children like to do in different play areas or zones (e.g., "What do you like to do in the sand area?" "What do you need to do that?"), or make statements such as "I noticed that you were interested in filling the bucket with hazelnuts."

ACTION PLAN:
INTRODUCING LOOSE PARTS

Play space where I will introduce loose parts:

____

- ☐ Identify and collect an appropriate loose part for the selected play space.
- ☐ Add the loose parts and any needed accessories to the play space.
- ☐ Stage the loose parts as an invitation for children's engagement.
- ☐ Present loose parts to children at a group gathering.
- ☐ Notice children's actions with the loose parts.

Adjust loose parts, if needed, to keep children's play going.

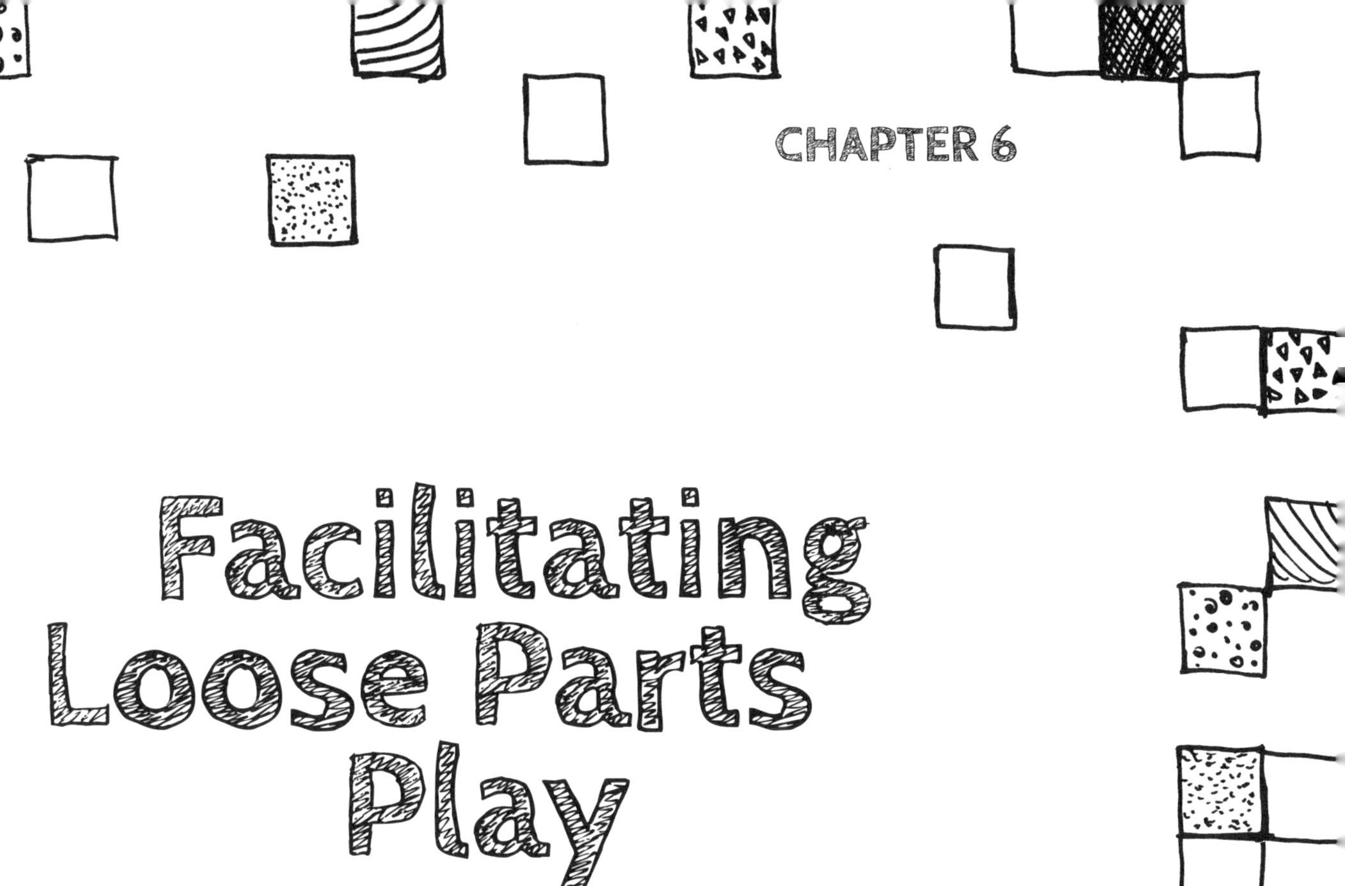

CHAPTER 6

Facilitating Loose Parts Play

An educator's role in fostering loose parts play is to prepare the environment for learning, support children's self-initiated play, determine children's interests, encourage and extend investigation, and make learning visible. It is important to be a keen observer, responsive to children's needs and fascinations and trusting of their capabilities.

Preparing the Environment

An early childhood educator has specialized knowledge about creating effective learning environments to foster children's learning and development. In loose parts environments, an educator also has loose parts expertise and is responsible for collecting, organizing, managing, and arranging them. Always keep children's interests, skills, and abilities in mind when carefully selecting and thoughtfully displaying each loose part. When presenting loose parts, make displays and materials exciting and enticing so that children keep coming back. Know the parameters of your space and let that guide how many loose parts to display. Exhibiting lots of loose parts sends a different message than putting out a few. (See chapter 4 for detailed information about displaying loose parts.)

Fostering Engagement

Engagement means the extent of children's focus, inquisitiveness, fascination, enthusiasm, and passion when fully immersed in an experience. In a well-prepared environment, engagement with loose parts happens automatically as children find them irresistible. Children do not need to be taught how to use them. They instinctively know what to do with open-ended materials and are intrinsically motivated by their possibilities. Here are some points to keep in mind to foster children's engagement:

- Provide long blocks of uninterrupted time for extensive exploration. Children need time to wonder, investigate, and revisit fascinations.
- Keep spaces flexible and materials open-ended. This opens unlimited play opportunities.
- Offer a wide variety of loose parts throughout the environment that inspire and engage all children.
- Provide large quantities of intriguing loose parts both indoors and out.
- Ensure that loose parts are easily accessible.
- Make sure that children have choice and flexibility in their desired ways to use loose parts.
- Allow children to transport loose parts.
- Offer accessory materials. Tree cookies may be interesting, but putting them with a balancing scale, sand, or miniature figurines may spark more possibilities.
- Let children pursue their own interests. Resist the temptation to direct play.
- Avoid intrusions. Children lose focus when someone interrupts their play. Just being close to children makes an experience special.

REFLECT

What environment changes have you made to support loose parts play? How have these changes affected children's play?

____

____

____

____

____

____

____

____

- Be responsive to children.
- Model and foster a sense of wonder. Be fully present. Embrace surprises. Demonstrate an inquisitive attitude to new ideas. Curiosity is contagious.
- Stay close, watch, and listen with genuine attentiveness. Your presence offers support and indicates interest. Notice and appreciate each child's engagement.

Uncovering children's interests requires investigation on your part. Be a keen observer of children's play, conversations, and activity to identify their interests. Watch for children's attentiveness, persistence, and total absorption. Observe their facial expressions and actions. Take note of their words. Search for insights that will guide you in discovering children's emerging capabilities and captivations. Close observation reveals each child's distinctive qualities, passions, and interests and directs educators in how to support and extend their fascinations.

REFLECT

What do you notice about children's engagement with loose parts? In what ways can you foster deeper engagement?

____

____

____

____

____

____

____

____

Thinking about Function

Actions that children do while engaged in different types of play determine the best type of loose parts to include.

- In imaginative play, children like to pretend cook and take on different roles. Loose parts such as glass stones or wooden rings allow for stirring and pouring. Scarves allow children to be an adult, superhero, princess, or pirate.

Check out a Discovering Children's Interests template at this QR link or in the appendix.

REFLECT

How do you capture children's fascinations, and how do you use that information in your planning to support and extend learning?

____

____

____

____

____

____

____

____

- In constructive play, children like to stack, build high, and create enclosures, so loose parts of varying shapes, sizes, weights, and textures that are suitable for building are perfect. Some examples include wood scraps, tin cans, and cardboard boxes.
- In sensory play, children like to scoop, pour, fill, dump, and dig. Coconut, abalone, and scallop shells make great natural shovels. Stones and larger seashells make wonderful treasure to bury and dig up, while logs and large stones support damming water and creating channels.
- In creative play, children like to design, make representations, and transform materials. Examples of good design and representational materials include small tiles, bottle caps, cinnamon sticks, seashells, sea glass, acorns, and tree cookies. Loose parts such as clay, sand, and water are excellent materials for transforming, as are design materials, textiles, and blocks.

Here are some good ways to begin capturing children's interests:

- Take photos of children's play for several weeks. Study the photos to see if there are any common actions. As teacher Cheri looked through images of children, she noticed multiple photos of Everett building high with a variety of materials and in different spaces.
- Notice children who often play together. What is their shared interest?
- Ask families if they have noticed their child repeating specific behaviors. Laura reported her daughter Annais's fascination with using unusual tools for mark making, including applesauce on the floor and lipstick on their white couch.

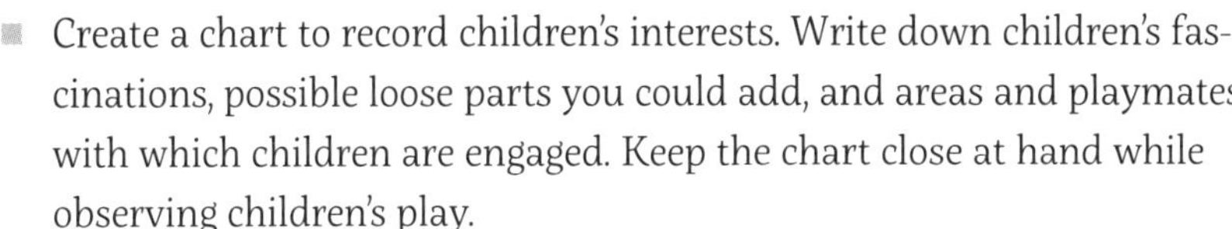

- Create a chart to record children's interests. Write down children's fascinations, possible loose parts you could add, and areas and playmates with which children are engaged. Keep the chart close at hand while observing children's play.

Here are some questions to ask when determining children's fascinations:

- What has their undivided attention?
- What experiences do they find captivating?
- What provokes their inquisitiveness, curiosity, and wonder?
- What actions do they regularly repeat?
- How are children responding to specific loose parts?

Another helpful hint for discovering what enthralls children is to look for what are called *action schemas*, or repeated patterns and interests in their play. Action schemas focus on ideas about movement in the physical world. They are typically easy to identify, so they are a good way to begin interest recognition. Characteristics of children engaged in action schema play include intense concentration, persistence, a sense of wonder, and deep enjoyment and satisfaction.

On pages 73–74 is a list of what to look for in action schemas that are commonly seen in children's play. This is not an exhaustive list but a good place to begin schema spotting. Know that spotting a behavior pattern and supporting a child's interest is more important than discerning which schema is happening. What follows is how I explained schema in my book *Transforming Your Outdoor Early Learning Environment.*

REFLECT

Observe children's play in various play zones and note common actions. Record your findings in the Discovering Children's Interests chart along with a sampling of loose parts (and a few authentic accessory items) that could support the actions. The following chart is an example. (See appendix B for a template.)

Check out a Discovering Children's Interests template at this QR link or in the appendix.

Discovering Children's Interests

Type of Play	*Function (Common Actions)*	*Flexibility (Loose Parts to Support Play Interests)*
Imaginative/ Dramatic Play	Mixing Pouring Role playing Stirring	Glass stones Maple rings Scarves Sea beans
Constructive	Building Creating enclosures Stacking	Cardboard mailing tubes Plastic cups Tile samples Wood fence post caps Wood pieces
Sensory	Burying Filling Molding Pouring/dumping Scooping Squirting Transforming	Aquarium gravel Buttons Corncob bedding Dry and liquid measuring cups Graduated cylinders Scoops (metal and wood) Wooden bowls, spoons, and ladles
Creative	Making designs Making representations Sculpting	Acorns Cinnamon sticks Colored stones Driftwood pieces Glass tiles Leaves
Investigative	Measuring Patterning Sorting Weighing	Measuring cups and spoons Pine cones Sea glass Seashells Tiles Washers

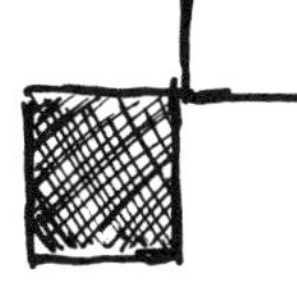

Transporting: Children with an interest in transporting like to move objects from one place to another. They may transport containers of water to the sand area or push a dump truck loaded with dirt or collect a bucket of natural materials. Transporters may also be interested in putting things in their pockets or being transported themselves, such as riding in a wagon. Loose parts particularly good for transporters include all kinds of containers and materials to move from one place to another.

Transforming: Children with a fascination for transforming like to change things to see what happens. They may add water to dirt, mix paint colors, or reshape clay. Dressing up and changing appearance, combining vinegar and baking soda, and rearranging materials to create new spaces are exciting experiences for transformers. Malleable loose parts that are especially good for transformers include sand, water, and clay. Design materials, textiles, and blocks are also good options.

Trajectory: Children who are captivated with trajectory like things that move through space. They may throw or kick objects, roll balls down inclines, or pour water into funnels or rain gutters. Their own bodies may be the trajectory object as they jump off high places, swing, or roll down hills. Loose parts that support an interest in trajectory include inclines and a variety of objects that roll.

Rotation and circularity: Children who gravitate toward objects that spin or roll have an interest in rotating schema. They may love to spin on a tire swing, make salad spinner art, or spin tops. You may observe children drawing circles, rolling hoops and balls, or watching wheels go round and round. Loose parts that foster children's interest in rotation include materials that are round or that spin.

Enclosing and enveloping: Children who are attracted to making boundaries around things find enclosing appealing. They may use blocks to enclose space and call it a house, garage, or zoo.

REFLECT

Observe children's engagement with loose parts. Record action schemas.

____

____

____

____

____

____

____

____

Children may also show an interest in enclosing if they paint a large shape and then fill in the shape's interior. Children who like covering and wrapping things may be attracted to enveloping. They may get inside hiding places such as a cardboard box, industrial pipe, or blanket fort. Wrapping up a baby doll or covering up oneself with a blanket are favorite activities of envelopers. Loose parts for supporting an interest in enclosing and enveloping include textiles and construction materials.

Connecting and disconnecting: A fascination with connecting involves joining things together, while being drawn to taking things apart focuses on disconnecting. Children who like to connect may use rope or string to attach items and tie things up. They may also connect pipes or hoses. Children who are disconnectors like taking apart and scattering materials, knocking down block structures, breaking sticks into pieces, or smashing sand castles. Loose parts that foster children's interest in connecting and disconnecting include rope, string, clay, sand, and pipes that connect.

Positioning: Children who are intrigued with positioning can be seen ordering and arranging objects by placing them in an exact manner. Objects may be lined up in order of size, shape, or color, or arranged in a pattern. Loose parts that foster children's interest in positioning include objects to stack and line up, such as tiles, bottle caps, buttons, leaves, tree cookies, seashells, rocks, sticks, and acorns.

Facilitating and Extending Learning

Once children's interests are determined, an educator's task is to place loose parts in the environment to support and extend their fascinations. Remember that children's interests continually change and evolve. An educator's role is to facilitate the learning process and not control it. Children's skills and knowledge are revealed as they play with loose parts. This can be an ideal time to scaffold and expand children's learning.

Here are some good ways to begin:

- *Provide opportunities for children to practice their interests.* The first step to get better at something is to use the skill. Getting good at pouring, throwing, mixing, or climbing takes time and effort. Placing loose parts in the environment related to a child's interest allows the child

to practice and become more and more competent. Be creative in discovering additional ways for children to repeat actions. For example, for children who are fascinated with connecting, add loose parts that support this interest, such as pieces of rope, shoelaces, and zip ties.

- *Build on children's play or interests by adding unique loose parts related to their fascinations.* Providing a mixture of familiarity and novelty will hold children's engagement. Even simple additions can extend play. For example, offering paint for children to add to water play or introducing water to the sand area will attract children who have an interest in transforming. Setting up syringes and squirt bottles with water will appeal to children drawn to trajectory.
- *Plan for children who have common interests.* When you plan for one child, other children who have similar interests will be compelled to join the play. Friendships often develop over shared interests like mixing potions.
- *Extend children's interests by making experiences more complex.* Suspending a hoop from a tree branch for children to throw balls through or providing spray bottles to squirt a target are more challenging for children attracted to trajectory. Vary the dimensions of the targets, as well as target location and type, to create more intrigue.
- *Provide variety.* Different loose parts are good for different things. The greater the diversity of loose parts, the greater the possibilities. Consider clay. Children love to feel clay and form shapes they can roll, flatten, twist, and squeeze. After children have had many opportunities to

REFLECT

How do you currently set up loose parts experiences that are rich in provocations and encourage innovation, imagination, and discovery? In what new ways could you set up experiences in the future?

____

____

____

____

____

____

____

____

explore clay with their hands, adding diverse materials such as shells, sticks, and dowels stimulates new possibilities.

- *Invite children to help each other.* Children's knowledge is a result of direct experiences with the environment and input from others. They can do many different tasks and welcome a chance to demonstrate their expertise and assist others. Encourage children to offer each other guidance, for example, in building a sand castle that does not collapse or constructing a sturdy foundation for a block tower.
- *Repeat or clarify children's words.* Restating words encourages conversation and engagement. It lets children know that you heard them, that their words are worth repeating, and that you are interested in them and their play. Clarification gives children an opportunity to let you know if you have misinterpreted their words and lets them further articulate their thoughts in words.
- *Ask children to explain what they are doing.* Engaging children in meaningful, natural conversation provides valuable information about their thinking and understanding. It also gives insight into next steps for extending their learning.
- *Ask questions that encourage thinking.* Avoid closed questions that result in a yes/no or one-word response. Instead, ask open-ended questions that have multiple responses and foster thinking. Helpful questions include: "What might happen if . . . ?" "Is there another way to . . . ?" "How did you . . . ?" "How could you . . . ?"

REFLECT

How do you document children's learning to reveal progress, thinking, ideas, and relationships? What new steps could you take to document children's learning in the future?

____

____

____

____

____

____

____

____

Documenting Learning

Documentation is tangible and visual evidence of children's work in progress. It may include photos, transcripts of children's conversations and comments, samples of children's drawings and artwork, and teacher and family reflections. Effective, meaningful documentation reveals children's progress, thinking, ideas, and relationships and conveys how young children learn. It is a way for educators to communicate children's learning with families, colleagues, and the public. It captures children's growth and development, offers insights into children's thinking, and serves as a resource for future planning.

Here are some thoughts about collecting evidence of children's play with loose parts:

- Focus on children's engagement.
- Capture photographs and anecdotal notes demonstrating children's sustained interactions with loose parts. Take candid photographs that reflect children's engagement and progression.
- Avoid interrupting children while collecting documentation. Getting interrupted from play means broken concentration and energy. It's hard for children to get back on track when they were deeply absorbed in play and are jolted out of it.
- Use documentation to notice children's particular interests, abilities, and repeated behavior patterns and to consider new learning invitations you can introduce.
- Collaborate with other educators and families to reflect on the significance of loose parts learning and how best to support it. Everyone brings a unique perspective.
- Use documentation of loose parts play as evidence to inform assessments. Children's learning in all developmental domains will be visible through loose parts play.
- Use documentation to discover how each child's unique strengths, abilities, and passions can be acknowledged, celebrated, and nurtured.

Remember that it is not the amount or visual appeal of documentation that matter most but rather how the documentation is used. The goal is to capture meaningful evidence that reflects children's understandings, learning dispositions, and skills and how this information may serve as a catalyst for deepening learning.

CHAPTER 7

Frequently Asked Questions

This chapter includes questions I hear often when mentoring educators and conducting professional development trainings.

How Do I Introduce Loose Parts?

Loose parts are well-chosen open-ended learning materials. Start little by little and add loose parts slowly. Introduce larger loose parts first—a limited number of the same item. For example, introduce a package of twenty to twenty-five disposable plastic cups for stacking in the block area. Add more cups as children become competent in using them and need more for complex building. Add another loose part when children seem ready for an additional challenge. This could be another stackable loose part, such as cardboard boxes, empty metal paint cans with lids, or another building item. Gradually increase the quantity of loose parts so that you and the children do not become overwhelmed. Use this same strategy for other learning spaces. Chapter 5 contains several ideas for introducing loose parts.

How Do I Store Loose Parts?

Loose parts are organized and displayed in every play area throughout the indoor and outdoor environments. Just like blocks, these familiar and unusual materials remain in the environment all the time. Chapter 3 contains multiple ideas for collecting and storing loose parts.

What If Children Do Not Play with the Loose Parts?

One time I observed a child who approached the water table and asked, "How do I do this?" His comment caught me off guard, as water play seemed so natural to me. I quickly remembered that he had previously attended a program where teachers directed children's play. Don't assume that all children know how to use materials. They may not have had many experiences with open-ended play.

Some children may not naturally know what to do with loose parts, and this can be discouraging when educators are excited and have spent a lot of time, energy, and effort getting started. Uncertainty is common for children who are used to self-correcting or playing with prescribed toys that have a specific way to be used. There is not a right or wrong way to use loose parts, and that open-ended nature may be unsettling to some children at first.

Here are some tips for supporting children who are hesitant to use loose parts:

- *Give time.* Have you ever moved, changed jobs, or gotten a new piece of technology? Even adapting to positive change can take time. Children need a lot of time to investigate, explore, and discover on their own. They are full of ideas and will explore them if given an opportunity to do so. Be patient and don't give up. Leave out the loose parts for several weeks and watch what happens over time.
- *Stage loose parts to inspire ideas.* Being faced with an unknown material may be intimidating. Have you ever stared at a lump of clay, blank canvas, or wood pieces and not known where to begin? Setting up an inspiration can spark the imagination and show a sense of what is possible. The thought is to give an idea on how to get started. For example,

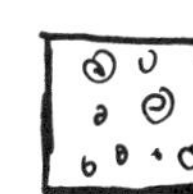

make facial features inside a picture frame with random loose parts, and then encourage children to make their own face. They may imitate what you have done at first, so provide encouragement for them to change their work. Ask, "What might you do differently?" or "How else could you . . . ?"

- *Encourage tinkering with loose parts.* As children play with loose parts, new possibilities emerge. Stacking tree cookies may start as a mindless action and transform into constructing a building. Placing acorns in a bowl may start as aimless filling and extend to pretend cooking of pasta.
- *Prepare children.* Before placing loose parts in the environment, introduce them to children. Chapter 5 contains several tips for introducing loose parts.

How Do I Encourage Cleanup?

Cleanup begins with environment design, loose parts selection, and loose parts presentation. The goal is to create a classroom that works well for children and educators—one that is well-functioning and easy to maintain with organized materials. It is a place where children feel ownership and take responsibility for maintaining it. Simplicity is key.

After every play session, arrange materials in a neat way so play zones remain organized and ready for the next use. Tidying up takes less time than you might imagine, likely only five to ten minutes with children's help. Investing a few minutes each day will save long, arduous cleanup periods later if tasks have accumulated over days or weeks. It also helps keep materials in good shape and lets you know when materials need replacing, repairing, or removing.

Here are some tips to help with cleanup:

- Limit the quantity of loose parts. Baskets overflowing with loose parts can be a disaster. They call out to children, "Dump me!" as children find something so irresistible and satisfying about dumping. To avoid this temptation and make cleanup more manageable, start off with larger loose parts as well as shallow baskets that hold smaller quantities of loose parts.

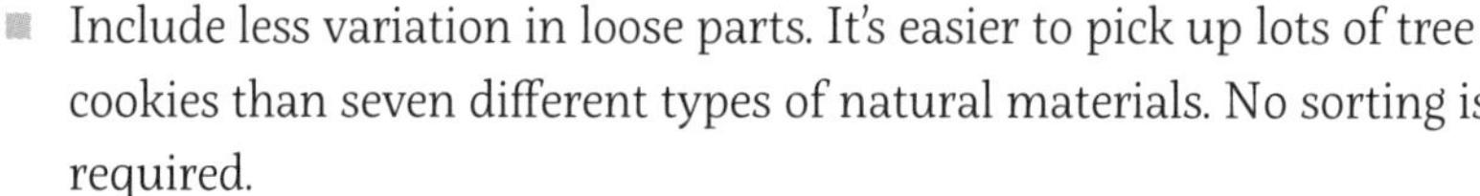

- Include less variation in loose parts. It's easier to pick up lots of tree cookies than seven different types of natural materials. No sorting is required.
- Consider placing one type of loose part in each play area. Having too many options at first can be overwhelming for children. Give them time to adjust to one loose part per play zone and learn how to put it away before introducing more.
- Allow flexibility in where loose parts are returned after play within the classroom or play yard. The nice thing about loose parts is that they usually do not have to go back to a specific area, and most work well in every area.
- Clean up alongside children. Be an active participant and role model in picking up loose parts.
- Discuss rules and routines around cleaning up after loose parts play.

How Might I Stop Arguments over Loose Parts?

The open-ended nature and flexibility of loose parts naturally reduces conflict since there are more play possibilities. If arguments are a challenge in your program, make certain there are a wide variety and large quantity of loose parts. An insufficient number of loose parts may cause conflicts among children. Some children need a lot of materials to successfully carry out their plans. The solution is to have enough. Having multiples of the same item can diminish conflict. Also make sure that there is enough play space. More arguments tend to occur in crowded, limited spaces.

What If Children Transport Loose Parts?

Remember that transporting is a schema. Children like to collect and carry objects from one place to another in pockets, containers, buckets, baskets, and wagons. The best advice is to be flexible and provide containers and materials for transporting. One way to limit the number of loose parts that are

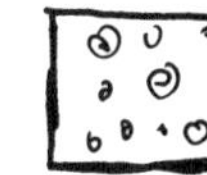

transported is to have intriguing loose parts prevalent throughout indoor and outdoor play zones. Children often go looking for loose parts or take them to another area because they do not have what they need where they are playing. If there are interesting loose parts in the dramatic play area already, then there is no need to bring them over from the art area.

How May I Prevent Disrespectful Use of Loose Parts?

I have heard educators state that when a basket of loose parts was placed on a shelf, the children just dumped it out. There may be multiple reasons for this. Here are some ideas:

- If the container is too deep or contains lots of different items, children may dump out the contents to see what there is or find something specific. The solution is to use shallow containers or containers with dividers to house various loose parts. This way materials are visible.
- Children may use loose parts inappropriately—with behaviors such as throwing, banging, or breaking—because they are unfamiliar and they do not know how to use them. In some instances, a child may do an action to determine the most interesting aspect of the loose part. Here are some suggestions to encourage more appropriate use:
    - Introduce the loose part by pairing it with an accessory. This offers a child an implied use. For example, place glass stones in a bowl with a spoon to suggest stirring or mixing. Place balls next to an incline.
    - Determine whether the behavior is a schema or developmental. Do not be quick to label what you consider to be misuse of loose parts as negative. For example, children may dump loose parts because they have an interest in trajectory and enjoy watching things topple out. Place items in the environment to satisfy their trajectory need by providing items such as measuring cups, scoops, and funnels in the sand table for pouring.
    - Model use of loose parts.

How Often Do I Need to Rotate Loose Parts?

Loose parts stay out all the time. Because of their nonprescriptive nature, there is not a need to rotate them. Children use them every day in new and exciting ways. Think of areas in your classroom where materials stay out all year long. You wouldn't think of putting blocks, dolls, or easel painting away after a month. These materials are always accessible. This same concept applies to loose parts. If children seem no longer interested in using specific loose parts, consider moving them to another area or adding another loose part to encourage new possibilities. For example, place an unusual building material such as corrugated cardboard with cardboard tubes in a block area. The one situation in which I may rotate loose parts is because of item availability during a season. In the fall, items such as acorns and leaves are abundant, while in the winter pine cones and evergreens are more readily available. If you are overwhelmed by too many loose parts in your program or facing organizational challenges, refer to chapter 3 for detailed suggestions.

Are Loose Parts Put Away after Children Play or Left Out?

In most instances, loose parts are put away once children finish their work so other children have opportunity to explore the materials. Items are returned to their respective containers. The more children experience the transient nature of loose parts and the cleanup process, the easier it is for them to dismantle their creations. They soon learn that the loose parts will be available tomorrow. There may be times, however, when a child wants to keep or continue their work. If this happens, capturing a memory of their work with a photograph may satisfy a child's desire to preserve their work. Another option is to designate a protected shelf or space where children may safely keep their work. Have name cards and "Work in Progress" signs available for children to place on their work.

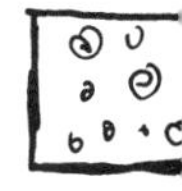

How Do I Clean Loose Parts?

Some loose parts are cleanable and others are not. The cleaning procedure depends on the material. Plastics and glass loose parts may be washed. Metal items may be washed but need to be thoroughly dried to prevent rust if not made of galvanized or stainless steel. Some textiles, such as fabrics, scarves, and napkins, may be washed, while some ribbons and yarn may not. Obviously, cardboard and paper products are not washable and need to be discarded and replaced when damaged. Typically, natural loose parts are not washed and are just replenished when broken. However, it will not hurt more durable natural items if you want to wash them since they are used to being outdoors and exposed to the elements. I put collected natural loose parts such as driftwood pieces, rocks, shells, and sea glass in a bleach solution as a precaution before giving them to children.

Always check the Centers for Disease Control and Prevention (CDC), local health professionals, and state licensing standards for sanitizing recommendations.

Suggestions for *cleanable* loose parts:

- Follow state or federal standard health guidelines for disinfecting and sanitizing materials.
- Some materials may be easily washed with soap and water in a colander and air-dried or washed in a dishwasher in a mesh bag.
- Nonporous natural items such as seashells and stones may be disinfected.

Suggestions for *uncleanable* loose parts:

- Ensure that children wash hands before and after contact with uncleanable materials.
- Discard and replenish items such as unfinished wood, leaves, and pine cones when damaged and grubby.
- Discard and replenish cardboard and paper pieces if wet, damaged, or dirty.
- Store items in a quarantine area for seventy-two hours.
- Create personal loose parts collections for individual children if necessary.

Do Any Traditional Early Childhood Materials Remain in a Loose Parts Environment?

The main objective in designing a loose parts environment is to create natural, aesthetically pleasing spaces by replacing plastic materials with authentic ones and exchanging static (one purpose) materials with loose parts. An educator may opt to keep a few traditional toys such as dolls, puzzles, and cars, but know that children are very imaginative in using loose parts to make their own interpretation of an item. It just might look different from an adult's image! It takes a lot more ingenuity to create a train track or traffic sign out of open-ended items.

Some traditional materials may stay. For example, an art area has mark-making items such as crayons, chalk, and paint. Glue, paste, and tape are not provided as materials are reused during design and representational work. Books are essential for reading areas. A dramatic play area has authentic pots, pans, and utensils rather than imitations, and a music area has authentic instruments.

How Do Loose Parts Environments Meet Environment Rating Scales Criteria?

Environment Rating Scales (ERS) are frequently used to measure quality of early childhood programs and required as a framework for continuous quality improvement. Loose parts environments score exceedingly high on most measures, while a few measures may require divergent thinking on your part. Prepare for an ERS assessment by familiarizing yourself with subscales and indicators (including space and furnishings, personal care routines, language and literacy, learning activities, interaction, and program structure). If you are using loose parts that vary from suggested ERS materials, consider how children's play with loose parts meets indicators. One approach is to make children's learning and development visible by showing children's engagement. Document children's meaningful experiences with

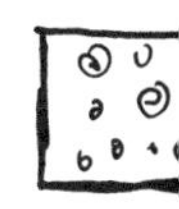

loose parts and their learning progress by displaying photographs, descriptions of play and learning, and transcripts of conversations as children play with loose parts throughout your program.

Since loose parts replace most traditional early childhood materials, questions concerning how to assess a loose parts environment often center around learning activities. Know that the learning activities subscale and items are only one component of the assessment tool, and there is a lot of flexibility in how indicators are met. More and more raters are familiar with loose parts environments and know how to accurately access them. If this is not the case, you may need to explain how the criteria are met, and in some instances you must feel comfortable accepting a lower score if you feel passionate about your rationale and the rater scores a specific indicator low. It is the overall program score that is important, not any single indicator.

The following are ways loose parts meet learning activities indicators.

Fine motor: Loose parts are developmentally appropriate and foster fine-motor skills. Throughout the classroom, loose parts afford children opportunities for grasping, stacking, inserting, holding, shaking, dumping, and manipulating.

Art: Art with loose parts is highly creative, sustainable, and allows for individual expression. Include a variety of loose parts, such as small tiles, stones, buttons, driftwood, seashells, and sea glass, for design and representational work. Offer three-dimensional opportunities with transparent cups and plates to stack on a light table, acorns and shells to supplement clay sculptures, or small boxes or wood pieces for building. Add mark-making materials such as crayons and chalk to satisfy a drawing materials indicator. Record children's art experiences through displayed photos and descriptions of their process and engagement. To satisfy a "relating art to current classroom themes" indicator, include natural loose parts found during specific seasons (such as pine cones, small stones, evergreen sprigs, and tree branches in winter).

Music and movement: In the music area, include loose parts that children may use to make sounds to satisfy a "many music materials" indicator. Incorporate natural materials that make shaking sounds, such as gourds and seedpods that contain dry seeds. Dowels of bamboo serve as rhythm sticks. Flat stones can be struck together like castanets. Coconut shells may be hit together like rhythm sticks or used to make the *clip-clop* sound of horses' hooves. Find instructions on the internet for creating numerous homemade

instruments using loose parts. For example, shakers may be made with secured plastic bottles filled with tiny washers or rain sticks with paper towel rolls. When making shakers, use nonfood items such aquarium gravel or small beads. Supplement loose parts instruments with authentic instruments from around the world, many of which are made from loose parts. Indicators for movement experiences may be satisfied by adding loose parts such as scarves, ribbons, and hoops.

Blocks: Indicators require blocks or materials suitable for building sizable structures. Substantial quantities of the following loose parts qualify as blocks: tree blocks, tin cans, countertop tiles, wood scraps and planks, plastic cups, tree cookies, and sturdy cardboard tubes and boxes. Accessories include loose parts that children use to represent people, animals, and vehicles, such as wooden spools and peg doll people.

Dramatic play and acceptance of diversity: Dramatic play spaces and diversity are viewed differently in loose parts environments than in more standard early childhood environments. Loose parts advocates believe that loose parts encourage more diverse, meaningful, equitable, and culturally relevant play experiences than the identified dramatic play materials in rating scales. From their perspective, theme- and gender-specific clothing limits play opportunities. While wearing a police outfit, a child pretends to be a police officer, whereas while wearing a scarf, a child pretends to be anything they desire: a man, woman, superhero, clerk, animal, dancer, or bride. Food props that represent specific foods from around the world may or may not be culturally relevant or authentic. A family's culture does not indicate the type of food they eat. Loose parts, on the other hand, are used by children to create foods prepared and eaten in their own home, which is much more meaningful and culturally appropriate. Whether playing dress-up or cooking, it takes

REFLECT

What other questions or barriers do you have concerning loose parts?

____

____

____

____

____

____

____

____

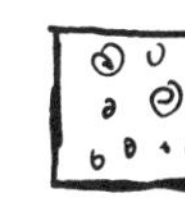

more imagination and creative thinking when using loose parts. In a loose parts environment, diversity criteria are met by providing authentic cookware, utensils, furniture, fabrics, artifacts, and photographs from around the world.

Nature/science: Loose parts invite children to experiment and practice scientific thinking. Natural loose parts help make connections to the environment. The following are just a few ways that loose parts support nature and science learning:

- Natural objects: variety of pine cones, rocks, seashells, leaves, seedpods
- Measurement: balancing scales and rulers paired with loose parts to weigh and measure
- Light: light table with clear and colored transparent cups, bowls, plates
- Magnets: magnets with loose parts that are magnetic and nonmagnetic
- Natural habitats: small worlds (miniature playscapes) of various habitats and animals

Math materials: Loose parts foster mathematical knowledge as children use them for counting, patterning, ordering, classifying, comparing, forming shapes, and measuring. Examples include bottle caps, glass stones, leaves, acorns, seashells, sea glass, twigs, polished stones, and pine cones. All loose parts have shape, whether it be geometric or organic.

APPENDIX A

Family Letter Template

Below is a letter to family members requesting loose parts donations. Use the template and adapt it to your specific requests. Consider adding photos of loose parts to give family members a visual image of requests.

Dear Families,
We are beginning a collection program to reuse, upcycle, and repurpose materials that children may use in their play. Reusing is good for the environment, and repurposed materials are free and challenge children to think creatively about how to use them.

These materials are called *loose parts*. Loose parts are open-ended materials that children can use in countless ways. Their nondescript nature allows children to decide what they are and their purpose. The very nature of loose parts is flexibility and unlimited possibilities. They may be investigated, transported, transformed, combined, and manipulated. They may be used for creating, designing, representing, pretending, constructing, exploring, and patterning. Having different types of loose parts easily accessible in each play zone affords diverse play opportunities and appeals to children's varying interests. When children are presented with loose parts and flexible furnishings, they engage in a wide variety of rich experiences that cultivate their learning and development.

Please see our lists of requested items below. You may drop off any loose parts to donate in the collection box located ______________. Make certain that all items are safe for children, and clean loose parts (for example, rinse out cans) before donating them. If you have any questions, feel free to ask a teacher.

We look forward to infusing these interesting materials into play spaces and watching children's engagement.

Thank you for your support.

Warm regards,

Indoor Loose Parts List

- Corks
- Floor samples (wood, laminate, tile, stone)
- Metal and plastic jar lids
- Plastic bottle caps
- Pine cones
- Seashells and sea glass
- Textiles (such as fabric, ribbon, string, yarn)
- Tin cans (with smooth edges)

Outdoor Loose Parts List

- Crates
- Driftwood
- Logs
- Stones (large)
- Sycamore balls
- Tires
- Tree cookies
- Tree rounds
- Wood cable reels
- Wood planks

Download the Family Letter Template via this QR code or going to redleafpress.org/lpa/app-a.pdf

APPENDIX B

Discovering Children's Interests

Discovering Children's Interests		
Type of Play	*Function (Common Actions)*	*Flexibility (Loose Parts to Support Play Interests)*
Imaginative/ Dramatic Play	Mixing Pouring Role-playing Stirring	
Constructive	Building Creating enclosures Stacking	
Sensory	Burying Filling Molding Pouring/dumping Scooping Squirting Transforming	
Creative	Making designs Making representations Sculpting	
Investigative	Measuring Patterning Sorting Weighing	

Download Discovering Children's Interests
via this QR code or going to
redleafpress.org/lpa/app-b.pdf

APPENDIX C

Loose Parts Indoor Inventory List

Art Area Loose Parts

- ❑ Colored paper swatches (card stock in varying sizes)
- ❑ Colored stones
- ❑ Floor samples (wood, laminate, tile, stone)
- ❑ Glass tiles
- ❑ Natural materials (such as seashells, sea glass, driftwood, acorns, leaves, pine cones, cinnamon sticks, small stones, seedpods)
- ❑ Plastic bottle caps
- ❑ Textiles (such as fabric, ribbon, string, yarn)

Art Area Containers

- ❑ Baby food jars/small mason jars (for water/liquid watercolor)
- ❑ Bamboo boxes (cutlery boxes—drawer organizers)
- ❑ Candle holders (metal) to hold crayons
- ❑ Divided containers for design loose parts
- ❑ Glass bowls (small) to hold stones
- ❑ Wicker baskets (shallow)
- ❑ Wooden and metal bowls (small)

Art Accessories

- ❑ Acrylic mirrors (12" x 12")
- ❑ Chalk
- ❑ Crayons
- ❑ Paint swatches (variegated color: red, blue, yellow, orange, green, purple, black, white, brown)
- ❑ Picture frames
- ❑ Plates, trays, placements, tiles (solid color for design work)
- ❑ Scissors
- ❑ Watercolor pencils
- ❑ Wooden cutting boards for design work

Clay Station Loose Parts

- ❑ Acorns
- ❑ Clay
- ❑ Clay tools (basic pottery tool set)
- ❑ Combs
- ❑ Craft sticks/sticks
- ❑ Eucalyptus pods
- ❑ Nuts, bolts, washers
- ❑ Old toothbrushes
- ❑ Seashells
- ❑ Sponges
- ❑ Stones
- ❑ Wire
- ❑ Wooden beads (large)

Clay Station Accessories and Containers

- ❑ Bamboo boxes (to hold tools—6" to 8" in height)
- ❑ Ceramic/wooden bowls (for water)
- ❑ Clay boards (12" x 12" wood covered in canvas)
- ❑ Sealed container (to hold clay)
- ❑ Wood cutting boards
- ❑ Wooden crates (8" x 12" approximate)

Light Table Loose Parts

- ❑ Driftwood pieces
- ❑ Geodes
- ❑ Glass stones
- ❑ Reusable ice cubes
- ❑ Sand or kinetic sand
- ❑ Sea glass
- ❑ Seashells
- ❑ Translucent colored containers
- ❑ Translucent colored cups and bowls
- ❑ Translucent colored cylinders
- ❑ Translucent colored tiles and stones
- ❑ Water beads

Light Table Containers

- ❑ Acrylic boxes, bins, trays, organizers
- ❑ Acrylic makeup, jewelry, and food storage organizers
- ❑ Quilting mirrors (for previewing patterns)
- ❑ Trifold tabletop mirror

Download the Indoor Inventory List via this QR code or going to redleafpress.org/lpa/app-c.pdf

Sensory Area Loose Parts (Sand/Water)

- Driftwood pieces
- Jurassic sand
- Seashells
- Shells (abalone, scallop, coconut)
- Stones (small and large)

Sensory Area Fill-and-Empty Materials

- Buckets
- Containers with narrow openings
- Containers with wide openings
- Cream pitchers (metal)
- Dry measuring cups
- Graduated cylinders
- Ladles
- Liquid measuring cups
- Metal buckets
- Scoops (metal and wood)
- Tin cans
- Wooden bowls, spoons, and ladles

Sensory Trajectory Materials

- Bamboo water pipe
- Basters
- Clear tubing
- Colanders
- Containers with holes
- Funnels of various sizes
- Pipettes
- Pitchers
- Rain gutters
- Sieves
- Spray bottles
- Squeeze bottles
- Strainers

Sensory Transforming Materials

- Dish detergent
- Ice
- Liquid watercolor
- Paintbrushes
- Paint rollers
- Scrub brushes
- Sponges

Sensory Rotating Materials

- Egg beaters
- Water wheels
- Wire whisks

Sensory Connecting and Disconnecting Materials

- Clear tubing
- Connectors
- Funnels
- Pipe tubes

Sensory Natural Materials (good for sink and float)

- Corks
- Driftwood
- Rocks
- Seashells
- Twigs

Construction Area Loose Parts

- Balls (wool felted, dryer, wood, plastic golf and tee)
- Cardboard cones
- Cardboard mailing tubes
- Cardboard rings
- Cove molding (cardboard)
- Driftwood
- Fabric
- Inclines (planks, gutters)
- Plastic cups
- PVC pipe (black) (4" or 6" in diameter cut into 6", 9", and 12" pieces)
- Spools (wooden)
- Tile samples
- Tin cans
- Tree blocks and cookies
- Wood fence post caps
- Wood pieces

Construction Area Containers

- Baskets
- Wood crates

Dramatic Play Area Loose Parts

- Blankets (baby)
- Materials to represent food
- Acorns
- Buttons (large)
- Canning rings
- Cinnamon sticks
    - Glass stones (large)
    - Pine cones (small)
    - Sea beans
    - Shoestrings
- Small tree cookies
- Stones
- Tiles
- Washers (large)
- Wooden stones
- Scarves (silk)

- Tying materials
  - Bias tape
  - Hair scrunchies
  - Shoestrings

Dramatic Play Authentic Accessories and Containers

- Baskets
- Canisters
- Cutting boards (wooden)
- Measuring cups (metal)
- Measuring spoons (metal)
- Metal bowls (small)
- Mortar and pestle sets
- Place mats
- Plates/bowls/cups (melamine) or outdoor camp set (enamelware)
- Pots and pans (metal)
- Spice containers
- Straw brush (for oiling pan)
- Tablecloth
- Table runner
- Utensils (variety in metal and wood)
- Wooden bowls (small)

Math/Manipulative Area Loose Parts

- Acorns
- Bottle caps
- Buttons
- CDs
- Cedar rings
- Cinnamon sticks
- Corks
- Driftwood (small pieces)
- Eucalyptus pods
- Film canisters
- Glass stones
- Jar lids
- Keys
- Leaves
- Liquid amber balls
- Marker caps
- Metal washers
- Pieces of old jewelry
- Pine cones
- Pom-poms
- Sea glass
- Seashells
- Seedpods
- Sticks
- Stones
- Sweet gum tree balls
- Tiles
- Tree blocks
- Tree cookies
- Wooden maple rings
- Wooden thread spools

Math/Manipulative Area Accessories

- Muffin tins
- Sorting containers (wood or metal)

Connecting and Disconnecting Loose Parts

- Bark
- Clothespins
- Combs
- Hangers
- Jars and lids
- Nuts and bolts
- Ribbon
- Rope
- Scarf hangers
- Shoelaces
- Sock hangers
- String
- Velcro rollers
- Wire
- Yarn
- Zip ties

Inserting Loose Parts

- Bowls
- Boxes
- Bracelets
- Buttons (extra-large)
- Candle holder with holes
- Canning rings
- Chenille stems
- Coffee pod holders
- Colanders
- Containers
- Cups
- Dowels
- Felted rings
- Hair donuts
- Hair scrunchies
- Keys and locks
- Letter holder
- Maple wood rings
- Metal canning rings
- Napkin rings (wooden and metal)
- Paper towel holder
- Plate holder
- Puzzles
- Scarf holder

- Tin cans
- Tissue box
- Tubes/bowls/measuring cups that nest together
- Wooden rings

Inserting Accessories

- Paper towel holder (wooden and metal)
- Mug or plate rack
- Oatmeal containers
- Wood tissue cover

Science Area Loose Parts

- Buttons or small polished stones (many for measuring)
- Collections
  - Acorns
  - Pine cones
  - Rocks
  - Seashells
  - Wood
- Lavender or spices (crush in mortar and pestle)
- Tree branch cut in sections (for measuring on ruler holder)

Science Area Accessories

- Balancing scales
- Calculators
- Food scales (mechanical/spring and digital)
- Liquid measuring cups (8 oz. clear acrylic)
- Liquid measuring cups (miniature clear acrylic)
- Measuring cups (metal)
- Measuring spoons (metal)
- Mortar and pestle sets
- Rulers (variety)
- Scoops (wood and metal)
- Spice jars and spices
- Succulents or plants

Writing Area Loose Parts

- Business cards
- Envelopes
- Materials for making letters
  - Acorns
  - Small stones (natural and glass)
  - Sticks
- Stationery
- Stones with alphabet letters
- Tree cookies with alphabet letters

Writing Area Accessories

- Attaching tools
  - Glue
  - Stapler
  - Tape
- Clipboards
- Hole punch
- Scissors
- Writing tools
  - Crayons
  - Markers
  - Pencils

APPENDIX D

Loose Parts Outdoor Inventory List

Art Studios

Natural Loose Parts

- ❑ Acorns
- ❑ Bamboo
- ❑ Bark
- ❑ Catalpa pods
- ❑ Cinnamon sticks
- ❑ Corn husks
- ❑ Driftwood
- ❑ Eucalyptus pods
- ❑ Flowers (dried)
- ❑ Leaves
- ❑ Oak galls
- ❑ Palm tree bark
- ❑ Pine cones
- ❑ Pine needles
- ❑ Rocks
- ❑ Sea beans
- ❑ Sea glass
- ❑ Seashells
- ❑ Seedpods
- ❑ Sticks
- ❑ Stones
- ❑ Sycamore balls
- ❑ Tree cookies
- ❑ Twigs

Textiles

- ❑ Burlap
- ❑ Carpet samples
- ❑ Fabric squares
- ❑ Raffia
- ❑ Ribbon
- ❑ Shoelaces
- ❑ String
- ❑ Twine
- ❑ Yarn

Tiles

- ❑ Ceramic
- ❑ Colored
- ❑ Glass
- ❑ Mosaic
- ❑ Natural
- ❑ Pebbles
- ❑ Pool
- ❑ Porcelain
- ❑ River
- ❑ Rock
- ❑ Slate
- ❑ Stone
- ❑ Subway
- ❑ Wall

Metal Loose Parts

- ❑ Embroidery hoops
- ❑ Film reels
- ❑ Keys
- ❑ Lids
- ❑ Metal caps
- ❑ Napkin rings
- ❑ Nuts and bolts
- ❑ Rings
- ❑ Washers

Wood Loose Parts

- ❑ Beads
- ❑ Clothespins
- ❑ Corks
- ❑ Craft sticks
- ❑ Embroidery hoops
- ❑ Floor samples
- ❑ Napkin rings
- ❑ Picture frame samples
- ❑ Scrap wood
- ❑ Thread spools

Plastic Loose Parts

- ❑ Beads
- ❑ Bottle caps
- ❑ CD cases
- ❑ Coffee stirrers
- ❑ Corrugated sheets
- ❑ Cups
- ❑ Cylinders
- ❑ Film canisters
- ❑ Film spools
- ❑ Marker caps
- ❑ Napkin rings
- ❑ Pipe
- ❑ Pipe fittings
- ❑ Tape reels
- ❑ Tubes
- ❑ Zip ties

Sound Gardens

Sound-Making Loose Parts and Accessories

- ❑ Baking sheets
- ❑ Baking pans
    - ❍ Angel food cake pans
    - ❍ Bread pans
    - ❍ Bundt pans
    - ❍ Cake pans (round)
    - ❍ Cannoli form tubes

Download the Outdoor Inventory List via this QR code or going to redleafpress.org /lpa/app-d.pdf

- Loaf pans
- Muffin pans
- Pie pans
- Roasting pans
- Springform pans
- Tart rings
- Tube pans
- Buckets
- Canning rings
- Colanders
- Cooling racks
- Drainage pipe (corrugated)
- Gourds
- Metal roof panels
- Metal trays
- Nana bells
- Pots
- Saucepans
- Serving trays
- Tin cans of various sizes
- Trash can lids
- Trash cans (metal and rubber)
- Wind chimes
- Wooden bowls

Striking Utensils (wood and metal)

- Bamboo pieces
- Dowels
- Ladles
- Mashers
- Mesh strainers
- Paint stirrers
- Pasta servers
- Slotted spoons
- Spatulas
- Splatter guards
- Spoons
- Sticks
- Strainers
- Tongs
- Whisks (ball, balloon, flat, sauce)

Mud Kitchens

- Canisters
- Colanders
- Creamer pitchers (metal)
- Dirt
- Mixing bowls
- Mortar and pestle sets
- Muffin tins
- Pancake turners
- Potato mashers
- Pots and pans (all types)
- Skillets and saucepans
- Spatulas
- Spoons (wooden, metal, slotted)
- Strainers
- Tin cans
- Water jugs with spigots
- Whisks

Large-Motor and Construction Zones

- Barrels
- Bed risers
- Benches
- Boulders
- Corrugated pipe
- Cove molding (2' to 4' lengths)
- Drainpipes
- Driftwood
- Ladders (small)
- Logs
- Milk crates
- Pallets
- Platforms
- Pulley system
- PVC pipe (black) (4" or 6" in diameter cut into 6", 9", and 12" pieces)
- Redwood blocks (4" x 4" posts cut into 4", 8", 12" lengths)
- Rocks (large)
- Rope
- Sandbags
- Sawhorses (mini)
- Tin cans
- Tires (bicycle, car, truck)
- Tree blocks
- Tree trunks
- Wood cable spools
- Wood crates
- Wood planks (narrow: 6" x 8'–10' and wide: 1' x 6'–8')
- Wood scraps

Trajectory Zones

Inclines

- Cardboard
- Cardboard or wood cove molding (1', 2', 3', and 4' lengths)
- Carpet tubes
- Perforated drainage pipe
- PVC tubes (black, white, clear)
- Rain gutters (vinyl)
- Rubber base molding
- Wood ramps

Bases to Support Inclines

- Barrels
- Boulders
- Cement blocks
- Crates
- Pallets
- Sandbags (mini)

- ❑ Sawhorses (mini)
- ❑ Tree trunks
- ❑ Wood frames with dowels
- ❑ Wood frames with rope
- ❑ Wooden spools

Exploring Trajectory: Things That Roll

- ❑ Balls of all types (whiffle, handball, plastic baseball, ball pit balls, wooden)
- ❑ Canning rings
- ❑ Felted balls
- ❑ Hula-Hoops
- ❑ Maple rings
- ❑ Napkin rings
- ❑ Pine cones
- ❑ PVC pipe (4", 8", and 12" pieces)
- ❑ Spools
- ❑ Stones
- ❑ Tires
- ❑ Tree cookies
- ❑ Velcro hair rollers
- ❑ Wheels

Exploring Trajectory: Things That Pour

- ❑ Dirt
- ❑ Gravel
- ❑ Sand
- ❑ Water

Sand Zones

Digging Tools

- ❑ Kitchen utensils
- ❑ Scoops (metal)
- ❑ Shovels
- ❑ Spades
- ❑ Spoons (metal)
- ❑ Sticks

Natural Resources

- ❑ Abalone shells
- ❑ Bark
- ❑ Coconut shells
- ❑ Rocks (large)
- ❑ Scallop shells
- ❑ Seashells
- ❑ Stones (small and large)
- ❑ Tree stumps
- ❑ Wood

Sand Zone Materials

- ❑ Containers (weather resistant and in various shapes and sizes)
- ❑ Funnels
- ❑ Gutters
- ❑ Metal buckets (various sizes)
- ❑ Muffin tins
- ❑ Pie pans
- ❑ Pipes
- ❑ Ramps
- ❑ Sheets of heavy plastic for building lakes, rivers, and dams
- ❑ Sieves
- ❑ Tin cans
- ❑ Trucks, diggers, bulldozers
- ❑ Tubes

Water Zones

Fill-and-Empty Materials

- ❑ Buckets
- ❑ Containers with narrow openings
- ❑ Containers with wide and narrow openings
- ❑ Dry measuring cups
- ❑ Graduated cylinders
- ❑ Ladles
- ❑ Liquid measuring cups

Trajectory Materials

- ❑ Bamboo water pipe
- ❑ Basters
- ❑ Clear tubing
- ❑ Colanders
- ❑ Containers with holes
- ❑ Funnels of various sizes
- ❑ Hand pump
- ❑ Pipettes
- ❑ Pitchers
- ❑ Rain gutters
- ❑ Sieves
- ❑ Spray bottles
- ❑ Squeeze bottles
- ❑ Strainers
- ❑ Watering cans

Transforming Materials

- ❑ Dish detergent
- ❑ Ice
- ❑ Liquid watercolor
- ❑ Paintbrushes
- ❑ Paint rollers
- ❑ Scrub brushes
- ❑ Sponges

Rotating Materials

- ❑ Egg beaters
- ❑ Water wheels
- ❑ Whisks

Connecting and Disconnecting Materials

- ❑ Clear tubing
- ❑ Connectors
- ❑ Funnels
- ❑ Pipe tubes

Natural Materials

- ❑ Corks
- ❑ Driftwood
- ❑ Rocks
- ❑ Seashells
- ❑ Twigs